GENERAL EDUCATION

An Account and Appraisal

GENERAL EDUCATION

An Account and Appraisal

A GUIDE FOR COLLEGE FACULTIES

EDITED BY

LEWIS B. MAYHEW

Director, Evaluation and Research, University of South Florida

Director of Research, Stephens College

HARPER & BROTHERS, PUBLISHERS, NEW YORK

GENERAL EDUCATION: AN ACCOUNT AND APPRAISAL

Printed in the United States of America

A-K

Library of Congress catalog card number: 60-7564

CONTENTS

PREFACE

THIS book is an attempt by individuals long active in general education efforts to describe theory, programs, and practices which in their judgment have proven effective. General education is a term having different meanings for different groups of people. Yet as it has evolved particularly over the past several decades, a number of characteristic features have emerged which, when consolidated, provide a workable and a generally agreed upon definition. General education has also been criticized by people who select poor examples and generalize from them. This book attempts to consolidate widely accepted features of general education so that an empirically based definition will result. It also attempts to hold up for public and professional scrutiny practices upon which teachers in general education programs should be willing to have the movement judged.

The initiative for this volume came from the National Committee on General Education which is one of the two standing committees of the Association for Higher Education of the National Education Association. The Committee on General Education over the years has sponsored a number of books. Sidney J. French's *Accent on Teaching,* Melvene D. Hardee's *Counseling and Guidance in General Education,* and Paul L. Dressel's *Evaluation in General Education,* are examples. This book is one more in that series, and in some respects synthesizes ideas first brought out in those volumes.

The contributors to this book are persons with considerable experience in teaching, administering, or evaluating general education efforts of collegiate programs. At the time the contributors were invited to join in the enterprise, their institutional affiliations represented a fairly wide range of colleges and universities. Due to the normal changes which come about in professional careers, three of the contributors have become associated with the same institution. Dr. Sidney J. French, Dr. Russell M. Cooper and the editor have all joined the administration of the newly formed University of South Florida. The insights these men express, however, have come from a much broader contact than their present shared affiliations suggest.

The preparation for a book such as this has necessitated correspondence between the contributors and a large number of teachers and administrators active in general education programs throughout the country. Without the precision and detail with which these many correspondents have described their efforts, the various chapters could not have been written. To these correspondents, then, the authors all owe a real debt of gratitude. Without the willingness of the various members of the National Committee on General Education to discuss and ponder the various stages in planning a volume such as this, a much less adequate presentation and analysis would have resulted. Lastly, the actual contributors to the volume have made the work of the editor extremely pleasant, both through their willingness to accept the assignment and their ability to meet arbitrary deadlines. To them particularly the editor, both in his capacity with respect to this books and in his capacity as Chairman of the National Committee on General Education, gives heartfelt thanks.

Lewis B. Mayhew

June 8, 1959
Columbia, Missouri

GENERAL EDUCATION

An Account and Appraisal

Chapter I

GENERAL EDUCATION: A Definition

LEWIS B. MAYHEW
Director, Evaluation and Research, University of South Florida
Director of Research, Stephens College

GENERAL education, while not a new term nor concept (the earliest use noted is in 1837), has come into common use just in the past several decades. It represents one more step in the long line of changing educational patterns which man has evolved in an effort to keep education abreast with other cultural and technological changes. As has been true of other developments in the past, general education became a dynamic force in protest against existing practices which had become obsolete but which were still being widely employed and defended. Perhaps the clearest notion of what general education is or what it intends to be can be seen by noting those things in American education which have been severely criticized. Actually, the origins of the theory underlying the movement and the techniques for achieving its objectives can almost all be inferred from the criticisms of education made by educators, social theorists, and laymen.

Possibly the mosts significant factor in this regard is the unbelievable expansion in human knowledge which has come about in the twentieth century. Even in the middle of the nineteenth century, scholarly men in many walks of life could justifiably claim to know at least the elements of all spheres of human knowledge; by the middle part of the twentieth century even trained scholars could comprehend only the barest outlines of a tiny portion of what was known of the universe. This expansion of knowledge, coupled with an increasingly complex industrial society demanding many and varied skills from its people, resulted in marked proliferation of college courses. In 1829 the entire curriculum of Yale University was printed on one page. In 1955 two hundred pages were required to list the available offerings. Obviously no single student could study even a fraction of the available curriculum. And with the rise of the free elective system, which allowed students to select as their individual interests dictated, there was scant assurance that students would even elect samples from each of the major subdivisions of the curriculum. With such freedom to choose, with such riches of course offerings, higher education came to resemble an intellectual cafeteria with no guiding principles and with no means of conveying to students any feeling for the unity of life.

A second quality about which protests were made was the caliber of college teaching. In the liberal arts colleges in the early nineteenth century, teachers were very much a part of the total lives of their students. They conceived of themselves as responsible for the students' moral and spiritual welfare as well as their intellectual development. Teaching (and not infrequently preaching to) students was judged the primary occupation of the college professor, and for that matter of the college president as well. While there were always ineffective teachers, as Henry Adams has so clearly shown in his account of his undergraduate days at Harvard, such ineffectiveness was a result of a lack of talent—not a lack of concern with the responsibilities of teaching. Gradually, however, the complexion of American education changed. The German conception of the university as a center for scholarly research was transplanted to the American scene in the form of the graduate school. This, through its direct influence on the institutions of which it became a part, and through its indirect influence on the liberal arts college through the professors it trained, revolutionized collegiate education.

Research became the most satisfying, respectable, and rewarding activity open to a college professor. Nonessentials, such as teaching, which interfered with research were to be accommodated with the least possible expenditure of time and energy. Indeed many undergraduate colleges which were part of a university were tolerated because they provided the raw material for future graduate students and because they provided, through teaching opportunities, subsidy to graduate students and thus to research projects of the graduate faculties. Since the rise of the research-oriented university was associated with the growth in significance of the Ph.D. as a qualification for college teaching, the ideals of the graduate schools were spread over the academic map. Young men trained by graduate faculties picked up the conception of research as the highest type of human activity and carried it with them into the liberal arts colleges to which they moved. Wanting to make a name for themselves in research in order to qualify for university appointment, they drew farther and farther away from any but the absolutely required teaching responsibilities. Such conditions could not help but result in poor or half-hearted teaching by any but the most talented and inspired professors. The lecture technique became the most frequent vehicle by which the professor communicated the results of his own or someone else's research to relatively passive undergraduates. Outside of class, personal contacts between the teacher and his students became rare.

Early American education had been based on a psychological theory that transfer of training was possible. Indeed the mind was frequently likened to a muscle which could be toughened on one set of exercises in preparation for actual work on other completely different activities. The classical languages were offered as much for the disciplinary values of study of their syntax as for any substantive values. Memorization was good training for all manner of adult tasks. The limited, required curriculum made no attempt to train directly for the actual activities of the ministry or law because it was assumed that the rigors of moral and natural philosophy and classics would develop powers directly transferable to professional work. Gradually, however, experimental psychology exploded this belief. It was shown that study of German did not increase one's ability to learn French. Developed facility in arithmetic did not make formal logic any easier. The implications of these results for the curriculum were profound, and fitted right into the increasing number of courses. As one wag remarked, there seemed to be solid psychological ground for offering a course in baton waving for right-handed people and another for left-handed people, with second sections of each to provide for sex differences. Curriculum builders, not understanding the full significance of newer psychological discoveries, went too far in providing separate courses for different skills. They overlooked what was later to be found—that transfer was possible so long as it was directly taught for, and so long as there were perceivable common elements in the areas considered.

At least partly as a result of these and other conditions, the graduates of colleges and universities in the 1920's and 1930's did not appear in good light. For one thing the colleges were losing large percentages of students who enrolled. Some of these of course were lacking in ability, but more dropped out of college because it did not seem to be meeting their expectations. Those who did finish college did not seem to be appreciably different from people who had never seen the ivy-covered walls. College graduates did earn more money, but their reading habits, their citizenship practices, their use of leisure, did not differ appreciably from the rest of middle-class America. Clearly something was wrong if as a result of the great expense and effort expended in giving young people a college education, the only gain was a somewhat greater earning capacity.

Still another characteristic of the American collegiate scene was the fact that colleges and universities were not providing a common universe of discourse for their graduates. One of the strengths of the English Parliament in the eighteenth and nineteenth centuries was the fact that its members were all products of the same intellectual environment, hence had a common language, a common ideology, and a commonly possessed set of symbols and allusions with which they could communicate with each other. The American college in the twentieth century was failing to do this. In a university of 14,000 students, with a curriculum of 2,000 courses and the free elective system operating, the chances against any two students taking the same pattern of courses were astronomical. Husbands and wives who attended the same liberal arts college frequently found that they had taken only one or two courses in common out of a four-year curriculum. The results of such a system of education were doctors who could scarcely communicate with their patients, engineers who had no feeling for the arts-training of their wives, and psychologists who could not understand sociologists even in common conversation. If an important responsibility of education is the transmission of the cultural heritage from one generation to the next, American collegiate education appeared to be failing miserably.

The changing technological and social world of America revealed still one more glaring weakness. Each generation of Americans, from the turn of the twentieth century on, was finding more leisure time. The urban movement with its accompanying smaller families, the technological revolution with its labor saving devices on the farm, in the factory, and in the home, were freeing men and women from the burden of long hours of work. Yet the educational system was coming to be designed chiefly to train people to do specific kinds of work. It was giving no attention to educating man to do those things which commanded most of his time—being a member of a family, a citizen, and a leisure-using human being. Some readjustments in education were demanded if it was to meet the emerging needs of its people.

To rectify these and other conditions, theorists began to advocate, and some colleges and universities to experiment with, a new kind of education to which the name general education was applied. Early prototypes were created as early as the post-World War I period with John Erskine's course at Columbia. The 1930's saw a few more innovations as Robert Hutchins caused a revamping of the College at the University of Chicago, as Floyd W. Reeves carried the Chicago ideas to the University of Florida, as W. W. Charters led the establishment of a general education program at Stephens College, and as Alexander Meiklejohn tried a bold experiment at Wisconsin. It was in the 1940's, however, that the general education movement really began to gain acceptance as a possible solution to the educational ills everywhere apparent. These programs as they developed varied from each other in important regards. They each developed out of indigenous conditions and reflected the diversity that is American education. However, the main current of development demonstrated some common elements which can be called characteristic of general education.

Programs usually tried to provide students with the broad outlines of human knowledge. For this purpose interdisciplinary courses were developed frequently in the areas of the humanities, sciences, social sciences, and the communicative arts. Sometimes these would be simply surveys of the high points of a fused course such as the history of western civilization. Sometimes they would sample in depth a cross-section of some part of the western tradition. The "block and gap" system of the science courses at Harvard exemplifies this. Sometimes, of course, students were simply required to take several different courses from the broad field of the social sciences. The general pattern, however, was to create new courses which if taken in their entirety would give at least a panoramic view of what man knows.

The theorists emphasized the importance of the teacher in these new courses and a number of colleges expended considerable energy in trying to train their faculties to be better teachers. A few places, such as Michigan State University, made the majority of its appointments to the general education program full time ones, with full salary and promotion opportunities. Some universities set up doctoral programs designed specifically to train teachers to handle interdisciplinary courses in general education.

Most programs assumed, either explicitly or implicitly, that a measure of transfer of training was possible. Thus it was assumed that courses in the social sciences could develop habits and attitudes which would be applicable to the person's life as a citizen. The humanities provided experiences thought to have direct relevance for the leisure time of the adult, and the sciences sought to develop a method of thinking which could be applied to many of the problems faced by adults. All courses in general education claimed as one of their objectives the development of critical thinking ability which, it was speculated, could be used in all fields with equal relevance. Indeed, Dressel and Mayhew[1] argued that critical thinking could well become the integrating theme or thread of general education. Their thesis clearly rests on the belief that the methods of thought taught in a communications course can be transferred to a social science problem.

Almost every program or course in general education seeks to change human behavior. Indeed, the concern for stating one's educational purposes in terms of human behavior is distinctly related to the rise of general education. Ralph Tyler and his colleagues at the University of Chicago taught that educational objectives must be so specified before either teaching or evaluation could ever realistically take place. The impact of his thinking through the Cooperative Study of General Education, the Progressive Education Association Eight-Year Study, and the leadership of the College of the University of Chicago on general education, has insured this point of view an important place in the entire movement. While there are of course major differences between institutions, most programs of general education have listed purposes somewhat in the form found in the 1947 *Report of the President's Commission on Higher Education* or the Armed Forces Institute's *Design for General Education.*

One of these purposes, which characterizes many courses and programs, is an attempt to provide a common universe of discourse for students regardless of their field of specialization. Despite differences in course titles or texts used, there seems to be an implicit attempt to provide a basic core of knowledge with which all students are familiar. Mikesell[2] found that certain basic concepts such as that of revolution were taught by most social science courses regardless of whether they were historical courses, problem courses, or some other type. Michigan State University may be thought of as exemplifying the characteristic with its

Basic College. That college tries to provide what is basic or fundamental to the education of all men.

General education courses typically claim to educate for the non-vocational aspects of life. They purport to educate for effective citizenship, worthy use of leisure time, effective home and family living, and movement toward effective personal adjustment. They are based on the assumption that men and women need to have formal education to fit them first for the task of living personally satisfying and socially useful lives. Courses may try to do this through a study of great books in the history of western civilization or through courses in personal adjustment. But the entire general education movement as represented in theory and in practice claims this as its unique goal. Medical or engineering education has a clearly vocational purpose. General education courses attempt to achieve something else.

While the pattern varies, general education courses represent a tendency toward more requirements for students. Although some institutions seek to achieve the goals of general education through some modification of the free elective system, more seek them through prescribing a certain percentage of the students' time. This may vary from a completely prescriptive program as at the College of General Education at Boston University to something over a half of the curriculum at some Catholic institution or to a bare requirement of one course for some curricula at Drake University. This prescriptiveness prompts the most stringent reaction to the free elective system.

Part of the defense for prescription is the need to force students to explore at least the broad divisions of knowledge in an effort to enable them to make more judicious choices of fields for specialization. And this defense is fairly characteristic of a number of the better known programs. The argument runs that the free elective system was not really free because students were choosing to exclude things from their programs without knowing what they were doing. A free choice could be made with respect to science only after a student had experienced a broad course in science. Then he would have some valid basis for judgment.

These arguments seem to be characteristic of the general education programs which have been put into operation. This does not contend that these are ideal characteristics nor that they represent all of the characteristics found in programs labeled general education. Many programs and practices possessing a number of these characteristics would have to be judged ineffective and quite a few efforts possessing none of them would have to be judged excellent. It is to establish some acceptable criteria of effectiveness that this chapter is written—and in the expectation that the examples discussed in the subsequent chapters may illustrate the application of the criteria. By way of contrast, however, some of the qualities of general education judged weaknesses by critics of the movement ought to be presented. It should be clearly emphasized that the justice of many of these criticisms would have to be admitted even by the most sincere advocates of general education.

One major criticism is that general education is really a meaningless term since people define it in almost any way their fancies dictate. At Michigan State it means the program and courses of the Basic College, which differs in important respects from the General College at the University of Minnesota. At the latter institution the program of the General College differs appreciably from the offerings of the Department of General Education in the College of Science, Literature, and the Arts. At one institution the full process of stating objectives and constructing a new curriculum of courses specifically geared to those objectives has been followed. In another institution older courses are simply renamed and thus emerge as a new program of general education. Boston University, Michigan State, and to a lesser extent the University of Florida operate required courses. At Harvard the requirements may be satisfied by taking some of a variety of courses offered, while at Stephens College there is no requirement save a course in Communications. To some, general education is rationalistic, with students being given principles assumed to be valid. They are then expected to deduce from these proper ways of behaving. To others, such an approach runs counter to the ways they believe human beings function, and thus courses are so organized as to proceed from students' own problems to the making of generalizations on the basis of them. For example, at St. Xavier College in Chicago the general education courses are all theoretical at the first level with recourse to empiricism in the second year. The course in Basic Beliefs at Stephens College, however, starts with a listing of students' questions, analyzes them in terms of their experience, and draws on the historical philosophical principles only when needed and when they can be validated by student experience.

The theory of general education is similarly subject to varied interpretation. To some, general education is the older liberal arts in modern clothes. To others it is the liberal arts without the aristocratic connotations of that term. To still others general education is but a segment of the older liberal arts curriculum. Critics of course say, "And not a very good segment at that." At any educational discussion of general education the question always comes up as to what this particular group means by the term. Critics again suggest that psychologists have little trouble defining their area of concern, nor do engineers. They question whether there can be much validity in an educational enterprise possessing such obscure lines of definition.

A second widely advanced criticism is that general education is superficial, that it is "watered down," that it deals in generalities possessing no real substance. Frequently using the survey course as the arch-type of general education these critics show quite vividly how the sheer volume of information covered and the speed with which it is done preclude any lasting impact on the knowledge or understanding of students. Or they will suggest that the apparently undisciplined use of information from a number of fields to study one problem, leaves serious gaps in student knowledge and may further leave students with a feeling that they know a field when actually they don't. Another facet of the position is that teachers are forced so to reduce the essential content of a field for the sake of the general student, that the emasculated result does no good for anyone. The science courses have been particularly vulnerable in this regard, as they have had to reduce the amount of mathematics demanded of students taking the course. Many general education courses are vulnerable and well deserve the criticism. While most administrators of colleges having general education programs will claim that they do not offer survey courses, closer study of their curricula suggests that they do. The general education courses are frequently great catalogues of information hung together by some theory such as the historical development of the west, or man as a biological organism functioning in a physical environment. Even when courses possess some logic which removes them from the category of a survey course, the teaching of them sometimes places them back in the proscribed camp.

In a similar connection, not a few courses of the problem-centered variety seem frequently merely to rearrange student prejudices rather than to force them to examine their beliefs in the light of new evidence. Social science courses occasionally err in this regard with students thoroughly enjoying expressing their opinions but without being stimulated to do the study necessary to test their own convictions. Courses in communication skills, which attempt to teach a new field such as listening, do not have a tested body of fact and theory as yet (although this is being accumulated). As a result time spent on this topic seems to the student a great waste. They feel that each one's opinions about how to listen are quite as good as the next person's.

Some critics scrutinize the newer types of social science offerings and judge them to be lacking the rigor of more orthodox disciplines. Courses such as those on personal adjustment, marriage and the family, and effective living have come in for a major burden of blame. They are contrasted—to their disadvantage—with courses in economics, history, and political science. Learning about the American Constitution is seen as more demanding than learning about how a late adolescent meets and solves his problems.

An aspect of this charge of superficiality is the belief that general education courses attempt to develop intellectual skills before the students have sufficient knowledge. People, to learn to think critically, the argument runs, must first be deeply immersed in the substance of a field. Before one can invent hypotheses as to how communities develop, he ought to learn everything which is known about communities. Students should not attempt to explain the origins of the Carolina Bays unless they have had a great deal of substantive information in geology, physics, chemistry, and astronomy. In the humanities it is claimed that students should not be expected to handle the Greek tragedies until they have been grounded thoroughly in ancient history and preferably in ancient languages as well.

Joel Hildebrand, chemistry professor emeritus from the University of California, is a major spokesman for this point of view. He feels that it is unsound for students to be expected to apply knowledge in solving problems until they have fully mastered the field. He argues that rather than being allowed to use a bit of chemistry and a bit of something else, students should study chemistry alone until they appreciate in full its complexities. Arthur Bestor, criticizing the high schools, is caustic on the subject. He feels that the courses emphasizing life adjustment are dishonest in that they suggest that students can learn the hard substance of a subject while struggling with problems which bother their young lives. He feels that people can make adequate adjustments to life only after they have mastered the basic intellectual tools of language, mathematics, science, and history. (Mr. Bestor is an historian.)

And of course much of what such men say is warranted. In personal adjustment courses, students are sometimes given such things as the psychological mechanisms of adjustment (projection, repression, rationalization, and the like) with the implied suggestion that they can now use these concepts in analyzing their own behavior. Many students have been asked to use the information of the cultural anthropologists without knowing in the slightest the tenuous nature of the evidence that field has to offer.

Another criticism is that general education, by teaching generalizations, does not provide students with solid information which can become part of their intellectual equipment. Students are taught that the Church was the custodian of culture throughout the medieval period. They never come in contact with flesh and blood examples of how that was done, so that they can appreciate the magnitude of the achievement. They are taught that culture is that which binds men together without developing a feel for what culture is like. Particularly do communication courses receive fire in this regard. Students are taught to communicate without learning the grammar and syntax of their language—which make effective writing or speaking possible.

The validity of this, claim critics, is established by the fact that general education courses do not prepare students for advanced work in a specialized field. Rarely has a department of chemistry, sociology, history or in any of the other disciplines felt free to modify their beginning work on the strength of what students learned in a general course. The general education course in science seems just so much waste of time for students who are going to take more science. Students have not learned to apply mathematics nor have they even learned the nature of study in a specialized field by being exposed to a few generalities about it.

Of a different order of criticism is the judgment that general education is just a device for obtaining cheap education. By teaching science courses in which there is no laboratory work, appreciable savings can be made in the instructional budget. By arranging large lecture classes in which surveys of knowledge are presented, much greater numbers of students can be handled than if they were allowed to enter smaller, more specialized classes. Forcing all students into large basic sections provides a relatively cheap way of screening out inept students before they get to advanced courses.

And, as a matter of fact, economics has led a number of institutions to consider general education. A common course, taught with a detailed syllabus, can be offered more cheaply than can a number of distinct courses each requiring a specialist as teacher. General education courses typically have a lower cost per student-credit-hour than do courses in the specialized fields and a much lower cost than professional courses. Some institutions have tried to cut costs of general education courses still further by assigning only younger faculty members or graduate students to them. In several institutions the task of each new faculty member is to do his turn in the general courses before he is allowed to teach upper-level offerings.

General education spokesmen have claimed a major interest in improved classroom teaching but critics say that this interest is not reflected in practice. Teachers required to teach a fused course embracing not only their own specialty but many dissimilar fields cannot be expected to do a good job. The historian expected to deal with philosophy cannot help but be quite superficial and in the end ineffective in teaching a field foreign to his own experience. The biologist forced to tackle physical science is going to feel so insecure that the effectiveness of his teaching is bound to decline. The policy of letting young and inexperienced teachers handle these courses also results in less effective teaching.

Here again some validity to the claim must be allowed. At one institution students overwhelmingly endorsed the idea of general education. At the same time they judged the teaching of the general education courses as less effective than in the upper schools. The writer has visited many college campuses and asked students whether the teaching was different in the general and specialized courses. Invariably general education teachers are judged less effective because (1) they are teaching things they don't like or (2) they are not familiar enough with the material outside their own field. The writer and a colleague visited a number of colleges in the winter and spring of 1952–1953 and attended general education classes at each one. With few exceptions the teaching seen was pedestrian, routine, and no more inspired than that found in other parts of the curriculum.

A last criticism is that general education courses are not as demanding of students as are upper-level courses. Not requiring precision of knowledge they foster a careless attitude on the part of students. By dealing with generalizations they encourage students to think in generalities. By covering a wide segment of human knowledge they foster a false sense of knowledge on the part of students. By dealing with knowledge at almost an opinion level they inculcate in students a faith in their own opinions and a disrespect for informed opinions. Further, by the way they are taught and the lack of prestige these courses enjoy, students are conditioned to put off studying them until after all other work is done. Especially for bright students, the work in general courses seems so uninspiring that they don't work at it. Such poor habits of scholarship then carry over to more demanding courses.

There is some evidence to justify each of these criticisms. And people interested in general education need to accept the evidence when it supports a criticism. However, the views of critics must be interpreted rather carefully. Many times critics will utterly destroy general education as they compare it with the liberal arts or specialized education. What they have done, however, has been to select the horrible examples of general education and contrast them with idealized recollections of the best examples of an older scheme. It is true that a poorly conceived course in biological science, taught by an uninspired man whose inadequate training thirty years previously was in physics, makes a sorry showing when contrasted with a chemistry class taught by a man of catholic tastes, great human understanding, and impeccable scholarship. Further it is true that some graduates of an orthodox liberal arts program consisting of separate disciplinary courses were well versed in language, numbers, and the skills of reasoning and that many products of general education today are not. Neither of these situations establishes a case, however. It is only when the full range of various types of education are appraised in the context of the society in which they function—and of the goals of the students they attract—that valid comparisons can be made.

In effect this volume is holding up some examples together with the goals they seek to achieve. These examples are not judged as perfect but they are ones which we would call effective. In selecting examples for inclusion we have used certain criteria. We feel that these must be satisfied if we are to make the judgment that this is an effective practice, course, or program in general education.

1. *Does the program or practice affect a substantial portion of the entire student body?* General education has as one of its purposes the establishment of a common universe of discourse—a common heritage for a group of students. In order to do this all members should be subjected to approximately the same set of educational experiences. This is not to say that they must all enroll in exactly the same course. But if they enroll in different courses, each such offering should actively seek the same goals in ways which are discernible to students. In the classroom if a given exercise is presumed to have general educational value, it should affect most if not all of the students in class rather than one or two. If, for example, discussion is held to be of value, it should be so conducted as to embrace a large number of the students in the classroom. If counseling is an important adjunct of the program, it should be so arranged as to aid most students and not just the few who seek it because of severe personal problems.

There are many excellent educational activities which do not reach all students and some of these may develop values of importance to general education. At Stephens College, for example, excellent courses in studio arts are offered which undoubtedly contribute something of importance to the general education of girls who take them. They are not, however, examples appropriate for this discussion. The late Clarence Lee Furrow often said the best general education course he had seen was an agriculture course on the use of manures as fertilizer. Again we would applaud breadth of vision on the part of such an instructor, but we would not select this for inclusion in our group of examples. At the level of classroom teaching a professor might do a brilliant job in stimulating his top students to do outstanding work. If this stimulation did not extend to the lower ability ranges we would reject the teaching as not being general education.

2. *Does the practice, program, or course realistically contribute to broadening students' views of human life?* A program of general education should be made explicit to students as a means of showing them more of human knowledge than they were aware of. If it is intended as exploratory so that students may make

more intelligent choices for later specialization, this should be made clear. Further, the activity should provide a base from which students can move to these broader horizons. If a course in the humanities seeks to have students understand their debt to the Greeks, Romans, and the men of the Middle Ages, it should first help students understand where they are. If a course deals with the ways a small primitive society functions, ways of interpreting this information in other societies should be made apparent to students. If mathematics or foreign languages are included in the general education curriculum, they may be justified only if they help students see more broadly the way human beings can communicate with one another.

There is room in the college curriculum for other orientations. Courses in statistics can be taught with a view only to developing certain skills. Courses in history may be included which seek only to lay bare the origin of some historical event. Courses in zoology may appropriately be offered and consist in nothing more than a deeper knowledge of sub-human mammals. These may be excellently taught but are not general education. General education must constantly relate the substance being considered with its broader significance for human living as it is perceived by students.

3. *Does the program, course, or practice have identifiable aims or objectives which can be stated in terms of human behavior?* General education is pragmatic education which aims to make discernible changes in people. It typically attempts to move an individual from one stage of development to another in full realization of what is being attempted. The objectives of general education—whether it be a course or a program or even a small segment of a course—should be made explicit, and then realistic attention given to those experiences most likely to achieve the purpose. If a goal of gaining facility in critical thinking is stated, it should contain specifications of what people do who think critically. If development of a satisfying philosophy of life is desired, this too must be spelled out. General education is predicated on the belief that there should be a direct relationship between what

is sought and what is taught. General education further postulates that goals are more likely of achievement when they provide a definite rationale for the ways a curriculum is organized or a class is taught.

Emphasizing the importance of objectives does not imply that there need be a large number of purposes stated for a given activity. As a matter of fact, many courses and programs have erred through having too many, with the result that no *one* is consciously taught for. Actually one or two objectives in a particular course are about all that teachers can keep in mind in planning their work, and some six to eight are about all that are realistic for an entire program. A course in social science would do well to concentrate on inculcating a certain body of knowledge and developing such a thing as critical thinking instead of listing a variety of items such as developing habits of citizenship, changing student attitudes, and helping a person realize his obligations to society.

With respect to this criterion no clear distinction can be made between general education and other kinds of education. Presumably any program should have purposes and any course objectives. However, in practice tradition frequently rules in place of rational search for purpose. If a course did not have identifiable and used objectives, it could not be cited as an outstanding example even though the students in it were bright and hard working and the professor stimulating. If a program did not have stated purposes which were well understood by the teachers in that program, neither could it stand as an example of effectiveness.

4. *Does the program, practice, or course realistically recognize prior experiences of students?* General education theory is based on a belief that human learning evolves out of blending previous experience with new knowledge, skills, and abilities. It argues that whatever is attempted should bear a clear relationship to what students have experienced before. A course in the humanities would thus make explicit connections between students' own questions about the creative aspects of life and what was yet to come. A program would consider the kinds of homes and

schools from which students originated and would capitalize on the base these sources provided. Thus a college deriving its student body from a rural population possessing a relatively low intellectual tradition would be quite different in form and in substance from a college drawing its students from a large metropolitan area. A college drawing its students from all over the United States would necessarily be different from one serving essentially students from one state. Similarly a teaching practice would differ with the kinds of experiences students had had. If most of the students in the class had had intimate familiarity with democratically conducted classes, a student-centered class would be appropriate. Had most come from more authoritarian situations, a different approach to the problem of teaching would be in order.

One can make some contrasts here with other kinds of education. Courses in internal medicine have as purposes to develop a common facility in diagnosis. Thus differences in background are accommodated as quickly as possible so that the course can get on with developing standard techniques of medical practice. Many strictly substantive courses such as entomology, or introduction to geology, can be and are taught on the assumption that the students have had no prior experience which is relevant save training in the skills of reading, writing, and arithmetic. The goals here are simply to acquaint students with a new field of knowledge. The goals of general education are not so clearly discrete. For a course to be truly reflective of general education there must be an expressed continuity with the students' past.

5. *Does the program, practice, or course make explicit the mechanisms for achieving integration?* In part general education appeared as an attempt to restore some unity to collegiate education. The free elective system had allowed students to take just an accumulation of unrelated courses with very little attention given to what they represented in totality. General education rests on the assumptions that integrity can exist in the curriculum but that definite steps must be taken to achieve it. Thus in a program various institutional means must be present for doing this. The means may be a system of comprehensive examinations, a team

system of teaching, a course emphasizing a major theological orientation, or a senior integrating course. Similarly, within courses there need to be built-in devices to facilitate integration. Such a device might be an historical framework showing how a variety of forces have served to create modern man. Another might be a series of examinations, each one cumulative with respect to materials covered on previous ones. Another might be asking teachers from another field to present introductory lectures in an effort to show the interrelationships among fields of learning. Such things as counseling centers and residence halls ought also to use definable techniques for achieving synthesis. It might be that counselors should teach academic courses in the general education program or it might be that the residence halls could be used as laboratories for social service courses, for example.

With respect to integration the difference from advanced specialized work or professional work is clear. There is room in the curriculum for a course on actuarial science even though this is unrelated to any other subject. The advanced courses in the sciences, literature, or the arts can achieve these specialized purposes without giving too much attention to equally specialized courses in other departments. Thus the teacher of a course on Constitutional Problems Under Lincoln need scarcely be aware that in Psychology a course on projective tests is given. For a general education course in social science to be conducted without awareness of the work in the humanities would be counter to the transcendent goals shared by both.

6. *Is the program or practice based on a holistic conception of human personality?* General education emphasizes integration of its manifold aspects out of a conception that the totality of human personality is rightly affected by education. It assumes that man's intellect is so related to his body and his emotions that one cannot be affected in isolation of the others. Courses in science are designed to demonstrate knowledge but also to foster scientific attitudes. Courses in social science not only teach the methods of inquiry peculiar to those disciplines but also to affect the feeling of students. Courses in the humanities seek as much to

alter the students' feelings about art as experience as they do to provide them with tools of analysis and with substantive knowledge. The fact that counseling has emerged as almost a full time partner of general education is not without significance in this regard. It clearly recognizes that an individual's success in his academic work is demonstrably related to his emotions and that how he feels derives from reaction to his academic work. Further, the kind of general education to be offered is a result not of the traditions of a particular institution and the talents of its faculty nor of the desires of its students. Rather there is an interaction going on between all of these factors which determines the nature of the offering.

An army course in rifle marksmanship, or a college course on I.B.M. operations or materials testing, does not depend for their validity on such a conception of a human being. One can view a human as nothing more than an accumulation of conditioned responses and still succeed in teaching students to translate medieval French. One cannot so view students and attempt to prepare them for successful home and family living.

7. *Does the program, course, or practice view as primary its own intrinsic goals?* General education should not be thought of as preparation for higher levels of training. These are goals which are valid in themselves and the efforts to achieve them should not be contaminated by competing goals of preparing students for more advanced work. The entire program for example should be so constructed that students will have received a defensible education if they never take another formal course. This does not mean that such a program should not be of value to higher order courses. Quite the contrary—It means that those courses should build on or take advantage of what the general education program does. But the general education program should not be adapted to fit the desires of the various upper-level courses. Articulation in other words should be initiated by the upper level, not by the general education program. Similarly, each course ought to set for itself the most valid purposes it can. In science courses these might consist of teaching students to read and interpret sci-

entific information found in the popular press. To expect a course to do this and to prepare students for the detailed demands of zoology, chemistry, and the like for pre-medicine asks more than a course can supply. Again, saying this does not mean that a biological science course has no value for pre-medical students. But the specific needs of pre-medical students should not govern the biological science offering. In communications courses a research paper should not be justified because it trains students for upper-school report writing. Rather the communication needs of all students should be scrutinized and techniques developed most likely to meet those needs.

Introductory courses stressing the physiology of psychological behavior are appropriate in a sequence leading to a major in psychology. Introductory French stressing grammatical drill would be satisfactory for language majors. College algebra would be fine for those needing that skill or those going on into calculus. None of these would be general education courses no matter how well planned and how well taught.

8. *Is the program, practice, or course as well staffed and financed as other comparable parts of the institution?* If general education programs are to flourish, they must have strong administrative support. If the movement is to attract able young men who propose remaining with the movement, they must have their professional future secure. No program which assigned its general education teaching duties to graduate assistants or to the youngest or weakest faculty members could be classed as an effective program. No course which was less well planned than the best of upper-level courses could be accepted. No technique of teaching employed chiefly for extraneous reasons of finance could be cited as desirable general education practice.

9. *Does the teaching in the program or course reflect attention to sound scholarship, probing deeply enough into a subject to bring about significant changes in people's beliefs and a demand for students actively to practice the skills which are being taught?* A faculty which is not alert to the best thinking of the relevant fields of scholarship can serve only to bring discredit to

the idea of general education. Thus a program which heaps the teaching of a general education course on the already overloaded professor of specialized courses would not be adequate. The program must allow time for teachers to understand deeply the fields they are trying to interrelate. Similarly, teaching which superficially hits the high points of some field is not satisfactory. It is more consistent with the theory of general education for three cultural epochs to be studied deeply in a course in the humanities than for twelve to be described so as to give a panoramic view of the West. Then again a program or course must provide time for students to practice skills. If critical thinking is taught, the materials covered should be few enough to allow for considerable class time for students to do critical thinking. If aesthetic judgment is desired, then an hour spent in studying one painting would be worth three hours spent in a lecture about the principles of aesthetic judgment.

10. *Does the program or practice make use of what is known of individual differences among human beings?* No two individuals are alike. Unless this is clearly understood, a passion for providing a common cultural heritage or a common universe of discourse can lead one into an unrealistically rigid pattern. Each program should make some provisions for students deficient in basic skills just as each class should make provisions to help the weaker students. Similarly, each program should provide for the exceptionally well qualified students. This might take the form of acceleration, enrichment of courses, honors work, or some other means. Further, each program and especially each course should provide enough variety in materials as to stimulate a heterogeneous student body.

Again general education can be contrasted effectively with other types of general education. Advanced courses in professional fields can assume that individual differences have already been manifest in the selection of students into the course. It can be assumed that all students in a graduate seminar on research methods of history have a common background of study, somewhat common abilities, and even, within limits, a common purpose. No such assumption is warranted in general education courses.

11. *Does the program, course, or practice provide for regular evaluation and accept the need for periodic change?* This criterion is not limited to general education. All educational effort should be concerned with evaluation and change. However, we would argue that evaluation is an essential part of general education. Its rise as an important adjunct of education parallels the development of general education. We would argue that a program whose leaders did not make continuous systematic effort to appraise its progress could not qualify as effective. We would suggest similarly that courses and practices which were not scrutinized with respect to their achievement of the purposes for which they were organized were not general education. We would also reject as ineffective those programs and practices which were regarded as unchangeable.

Obviously no program, course, or practice can achieve perfection with respect to these criteria. They do suggest goals toward which general education can strive. They can suggest what effective general education really is.

NOTES

[1] Dressel, P. L., & Mayhew, L. B., *General Education: Explorations in Evaluation* (Washington, A. C. E.), 1954.

[2] Mikesell, Doyle, "Social Science General Education Courses," *Junior College Journal,* January 1954, 268–277.

Chapter II

ADMINISTRATIVE STRUCTURES AND PRACTICES IN GENERAL EDUCATION

W. HUGH STICKLER

Director, Office of Institutional Research and Service, and Professor of Higher Education, Florida State University

INTRODUCTION

FROM the vast complex of efforts to establish programs of general education we have selected a condensed summary of samplings only of what seem to us to be effective administrative structures and practices in general education. Other excellent programs must be omitted for lack of space.

In our sample we have deliberately selected a variety of institutions. Included are several large universities, public and private, state and municipal. There are state colleges, teachers colleges, liberal arts colleges, and junior colleges. Some are prestige institutions; others are less well known. It is our belief, however, that all of these institutions have programs of general education which may be described as effective.

In developing this chapter we have drawn on a variety of sources, some published and some in draft form, too vast to be mentioned individually. Also, a rich correspondence with responsible officials has been most helpful.

At the close of the chapter we attempt to summarize some of the principles of effective administration of general education which have been gleaned from the literature, reports, and correspondence.

LARGE COMPLEX INSTITUTIONS

Columbia University. One of the oldest programs of general education in the nation is to be found at Columbia College in Columbia University. At the end of World War I a small group of young men—Harry J. Carman, later to become dean of the college, among them—redefined the objectives of the college in terms of student needs and with the support and assistance of the then-dean, Herbert Edwin Hawkes, began to devise better curricular machinery for realizing these objectives. Through an evolutionary process covering many years (some would say it is still in progress) the general education program came into being. Contemporary Civilization, the first course in the program, was first offered in 1919.

At Columbia the general education program operates entirely within the college and does not apply to other instructional units of the university. Included in the program are both departmental and divisional courses. Typical of the departmental courses is the second year of the required humanities course. On the other hand, the general education courses in the social sciences and the first year of the required humanities sequence are divisional in character. The members of the social science staff are drawn from the Departments of Anthropology, Economics, Government, History, Philosophy, Religion, and Sociology. The staff for the beginning humanities course is recruited from the departments of Philosophy, English, Classics, History, Modern Foreign Languages, Music, Religion, and Fine Arts. In spite of its long experience in the field of general education, Columbia has never been able to develop and maintain over a period of time a satisfactory divisional course in the area of the natural sciences.

In Columbia College the entire general education program is administered by the Committee on Instruction, of which the dean of the college is chairman. Courses which do not cut across departmental lines are administered by the committee through the executive officer of the department. Each divisional course, however, is administered by the committee through an executive officer of the course. This individual is appointed from the instructional staff for a term of five years by the Committee on Instruction. He is eligible for reappointment. Assisting the executive officer of the divisional course is an advisory committee composed of one member from each of the collaborating departments. Neither the executive officer nor any member of his advisory committee can be a departmental executive officer.

The executive officer and his advisory committee supervise the operation of the divisional course. With the advice of the advisory committee the executive officer appoints committees to determine course content, construct syllabi, select texts, determine reading materials, make examinations, and the like. The executive officer of the course confers with departmental executive officers relative to personnel nominated by the several collaborating departments to give instruction in the general education course. No instructor is forced to teach in a general education division course against his will. Subject to the approval of his advisory committee, the course executive officer has power to reject any person recommended by a department whom he deems to be unqualified to be a member of the instructional staff of the divisional course.

At Columbia College there is only one budget. No funds are specifically earmarked for the operation of the general education program.

According to Harry J. Carman, now Dean Emeritus of Columbia College, the present system of administering the general education program ". . . works smoothly and is very effective."

Harvard University. After two years of study the Harvard Committee in 1945 issued its now famous report, *General Education in a Free Society.*[1] In the fall of 1946–1947 the general education program was launched in the Harvard College curriculum on a provisional basis. In March 1949, the faculty by an overwhelming majority approved the plan and voted to move the general education program from provisional status to an integral part of the curriculum. The decision provided for the introduction of the program on a required basis by degrees; thus only with the Class of 1955 did the entire plan go into operation.

Basically, Harvard College is committed to a program of general education as an integral part of liberal arts education. The essential plan is that a series of courses in general education is offered in each of three areas: the humanities, the social sciences, and the natural sciences. Instead of offering a single elementary course in each of the areas, several versions of the same course are provided, and the student is free to choose among them. From the general education offerings, each undergraduate is required to select six courses, three at the elementary level (one in each of the areas indicated) and three at a more advanced level. Although the required introductory courses must, in most instances, be taken during the first two years, it is assumed that students will continue to take suitable advanced courses in general education during the third and probably the fourth year. Harvard thinks of general education and specialized study as running concurrently through the entire undergraduate program.

No member of the teaching staff gives his time exclusively to general education; some work is always done in the department of his specialization. No regular appointment is made without the concurrence of the department in which the appointee's principal interest lies. In the case of major appointments, the candidate is recommended by the Committee on General Education and the appropriate department. The appointee may then hold a dual title—for example, "Professor of General Education and Chemistry."

The general education program at Harvard is simply administered. Basically, the program operates through the regular departments. The responsible body is the Committee on General Education which includes twelve permanent members of the faculty chosen from a representative group of contributing departments. The committee, whose executive head is designated merely as chairman, operates under the Faculty of Arts and Sciences. The committee meets monthly. Agenda items include such matters as appointments, promotions, the course of study, and machinery for operating the general education program.

Harvard's scheme for administering its program of general education seems to be working satisfactorily. In a letter to the author of this chapter, David Owen, Gurney Professor of History, says, "It is fairly clear, I think, that any drastic deviation from the pattern of administration that we have been following would be impossible to introduce here."

Boston University. Boston University has two separate and distinct programs of general education: one in the College of General Education (established in 1946), the other in the Junior College (established in 1952). A basic difference between the two lies in the rigidity of admission standards, particularly in that the College of General Education pays more attention to patterns of pre-college courses than does the Junior College.

In order to achieve its goals of general education, each of the two colleges has a completely prescribed curriculum. Unusual efforts are made at "total integration"—not only the interrelating of various disciplines into broad areas (e.g., physics, chemistry, geology, astronomy, and meteorology into physical science) but also the interrelating of various broad area subjects (e.g., physical science, biological science, social science, communications, humanities) into a total integrated learning experience. Results flowing out of the two colleges seem to indicate a considerable measure of success in this undertaking.

From the beginning, each of the two colleges offering general education at Boston University has had a separate faculty. Each faculty member is carefully selected in terms of the breadth and depth of his academic training and his suitability and willingness to do this kind of work. The teacher thereafter spends full time working in general education. Boston University feels that a separate faculty dedicated to general education work is essential in achieving its general education goals.

A feature of the program in the Junior College is the team approach to general education. In this scheme a team of five instructors from the five required subject matter areas (one each from humanities, social relations, science, guidance, and communications) bands together to teach the same students (about 125 assigned to each team). The goal is to facilitate integration among the various subject matter areas in the curriculum and to deal effectively with students as individuals.

The College of General Education was at first a completely independent instructional unit. It had its own full time dean who reported directly to the president of the university. It is still an independent instructional unit but the man who now serves as Dean of the College of General Education also serves as dean of the College of Liberal Arts. The dean of the Junior College administers only that one instructional unit. Each of the two colleges offering general education has the responsibility and authority to establish goals, select and/or construct instructional materials, elect staff, determine promotion and pay, and in general administer its own affairs.

University of Chicago. At the University of Chicago the general education program is vested in the college. Originally, general education was the entire business of the college. Carefully selected and highly able students were admitted, frequently at the end of the tenth or eleventh year in secondary school. The curriculum was a totally prescribed program of general studies. Students progressed by passing a series of comprehensive examinations in a variety of fields of general education. When all of these examinations had been passed the baccalaureate degree was conferred. Usually this would be at that point which would normally fall at the end of the sophomore year of college work.

In 1953 the University of Chicago decided to relocate and redefine the baccalaureate degree. High school graduation is now normally required for admission (which, incidentally, remains highly selective) and the curriculum of the college covers four years of work and leads to the regular baccalaureate degree. In the new curriculum a program of general studies is combined with concentrated work in a given discipline. It will be noted that the program now offered more nearly parallels those offered in the majority of senior institutions of higher education in the nation.

Effective in the fall of 1958 further reorganization was implemented. Although considerably expanded—approximately one hundred members have been added—the faculty of the college remains undepartmentalized. Rather, it is organized into four large divisions: biological sciences, physical sciences, humanities, and social sciences. Each division includes persons offering instruction in general education in the area, together with persons who teach the more specialized concentration courses in that field. There is a two-year prescribed curriculum in general education which is uniform regardless of the student's field of concentration.

At present the organizational structure for the administration of the general education program in the college at the University of Chicago is in a state of transition. To quote Robert E. Streeter, Dean of the College, "It would be rash to predict at this point how well this new organization will work. Since more than half of the members of the faculty have had direct experience with teaching in our general education program, since the College remains undepartmentalized, and since the College has a budget and the power of appointment, we expect to maintain the energy which is requisite for a general studies program of high quality."

The college at the University of Chicago has a long and rich history of experience in the field of general education. It may be expected that a high-quality program of general studies will be maintained in the future.

University of Louisville. At the University of Louisville, a municipal institution, the general education program was launched in the fall of 1933. It operates entirely within the College of Arts and Sciences and does not apply to the other instructional units of the university.

The basic program of general education consists of thirty semester hours of academic work: three six-semester-hour courses (English Composition, Modern Social Problems, and Introduction to the Sciences) in the freshman year, two six-semester-hour courses (Introduction to the Humanities and History of Civilization) in the sophomore year. In addition, the student must pass the Sophomore Comprehensive Test at the end of the sophomore year and take an integrating course during his senior year.

These senior integrating courses merit further consideration. As has been seen, the student works off his basic general education requirements during his first two years in the university. During this time, and increasingly in his junior and senior years, he is working on a major in the usual manner. Then as a senior he comes together with his fellows who have majored in the same division and takes an integrating course. The required senior course in the social sciences is called Great Social Thinkers; that in the natural sciences is called History and Philosophy of Science; and that in the humanities is called Principles of Cultural History. Each of these integrating courses is designed to serve as a capstone course for the entire undergraduate program.

As has been suggested, the College of Arts and Sciences at the University of Louisville is organized into three divisions: social sciences, natural sciences, and humanities. Every two years faculty members in each division nominate, to the dean, staff members for the chairmanship of the division. The dean in turn recommends his choice to the president of the university for the final appointment. Through this simple machinery—division faculties, the chairmen of the divisions, and the dean—the general education program has operated for a quarter of a century. According to J. J. Oppenheimer, Dean Emeritus, the administrative structure works well ". . . for our type of organization within the College of Arts and Sciences. Of course, if it were a University-wide organization, I think I would favor another kind."

University of Florida. Among state-supported institutions, one of the first to organize and operate a program of general education on an institution-wide basis was the University of Florida. The program there has been in operation since 1935.

Seven courses totaling thirty-six semester hours of credit constitute the general education program at the University of Florida. These core courses are American Institutions, the Physical Sciences, Freshman English (reading, writing, and speaking), Practical Logic, Fundamental Mathematics, the Humanities, and Biological Science. The university prescribes and requires this basic core of work of all students, regardless of their final academic destinations.

At the University of Florida the general education program is vested in the University College, an independent, lower division, two-year instructional unit with its own academic dean who reports directly to the president of the university. Within the University College the staff of each core course constitutes a department. Each department has its own department head, its own faculty, its own budget; administratively it is completely independent of other instructional units of the university. Although the University College employs its own staff, a sort of "lend-lease" policy is in operation. About one-third of the University College faculty is loaned to the several departments in the upper divisions, usually to teach one course each. The departments in the upper division in turn pay back with time from some of their faculty members. This informal exchange of staff seems to work well. It is to be noted that the training and degrees held by the University College faculty are equal if not superior to the training and degrees required in upper division units. Promotion and pay policies are the same in the University College as in other instructional units of the university.

The Board of Examiners plays an important role in the general education program at the University of Florida. It constructs, administers, scores, and interprets comprehensive examinations in each of the core courses and serves as the chief agency for evaluating the general education program.

The general education program of the University of Florida was recently (1956) evaluated by an outside board of consultants. Although the consultants offered a number of suggestions for further improvement, the general education program as a whole received a clean bill of health.

In a recent letter to this writer, W. W. Little, Dean of the University College, summarizes his evaluation in these words: "I believe the present organization is adequate and effective."

Michigan State University. Following a period of study covering several months, the faculty of Michigan State University in the spring of 1944 approved the idea of a program of general education. The program came into being that fall.

In this university the major responsibility for general education rests in an administrative unit called the Basic College. It, like the University College at the University of Florida, is a completely independent instructional unit with its own dean, its own staff, and its own budget. It enrolls all freshmen and sophomores, and—again like the University College at the University of Florida—serves all Michigan State University students, regardless of their ultimate academic destinations.

At present Michigan State requires in its general education program four courses carrying forty-five quarter-hours of credit. These courses are Communication Skills, Natural Science, Social Science, and the Humanities.

Integral parts of the general education program at Michigan State are the Office of Evaluation Services, which constructs, administers, scores, and interprets comprehensive examinations and carries on numerous other evaluative studies, and the Office of Student Affairs, which has developed an excellent program of student advisement and an efficient record system.

Like the University College at the University of Florida, the Basic College at Michigan State University has its own faculty. Unlike the University of Florida, however, there is at Michigan State very little trading back and forth of teaching personnel between the Basic College and the upper divisions of the university. At Michigan State, teachers in the Basic College seem to be willing to spend full time working in the area of general education and related fields. Apparently they find rewarding professional careers in this kind and at this level of academic work.

The Basic College has made great strides forward in general education since its establishment in 1944. That it is ever alert to further refinement and new opportunities is shown by this statement of its dean, Edward A. Carlin: "We in the Basic College are at present actively discussing ways and means of introducing materials, concepts, and experiences into our program that will better equip our students to function in a world shrinking so fast as to be frightening."

Oklahoma State University. After long and careful study, and after an examination of all criticisms by friends and opponents alike, the general education program at Oklahoma State University was initiated in 1935. This is not a university-wide program on a required basis. It operates within the College of Arts and Sciences although various other instructional units of the university on their own initiative use portions of the program in their own academic work.

Within arts and sciences, general education is an all-department, all-college concern. Student orientation, advisement, and evaluation are all integral parts of the program which centers about five basic courses: Physical Science, Biological Science, Social Science, Humanities, and General Mathematics.

Standards in general education are recognized by both faculty and students to be high. There has been no disposition to assign weak or incompetent teachers to these courses. Rather, throughout its history the general education program at Oklahoma State has been able to enlist many of the most competent and most effective teachers in the institution. Professional advancement and salary considerations are as favorable for teachers in general education courses as for specialists working in any other area.

The administrative structure within which the general education program functions at Oklahoma State University is characterized by informality and flexibility. Some formal organization is discernible but it is held to a minimum. In this institution the goal has been to organize general education in such manner as to facilitate its integration administratively with the several major departments and divisions of the College of Arts and Sciences.

In its initial stages, the general education program was administered directly by the dean of the college. As the institution grew, help had to be enlisted. A Director of General Education, who functions as an assistant to the dean, was appointed. Under the director are an advisement officer and an examiner.

The Director of General Education works with problems of staff and curriculum through the General Education Committee of which he is chairman. This committee is made up of the chairmen of the several general courses. The dean is a member of the General Education Committee *ex officio*.

Personnel for the general courses are selected by the chairman of each course in conference with the heads of the departments concerned. In case of failure to agree, the dean arbitrates. New appointments bear the recommending signatures of both the general course chairman and the head of the department, and salary recommendations usually are set by joint agreement. A maximum of flexibility has been maintained, permitting professors to withdraw from general education into departmental teaching or vice versa very much as they choose.

Within this loose administrative organization general education at Oklahoma State has operated effectively for a quarter of a century. It is the opinion of the writer that the program has run smoothly primarily because of the personality and strong leadership of the dean. Whether with changes of leadership the program can continue to function effectively within its present informal and flexible administrative organization remains to be seen.

Kansas State University. Following a period of faculty study under the leadership of the then-president, Milton S. Eisenhower, Kansas State College initiated its program of general education in 1944. Basically, the program centers about four inter-disciplinary courses: Man and the Social World, Biology in Relation to Man, Man's Physical World, and Man and the Cultural World. Additional work is required in written communication and oral communication. Originally a program in citizenship training operated by the Institute of Citizenship contributed substantially to the general education program. The institute, however, was supported by private funds. When these funds were exhausted, the institute was discontinued. The rest of the program, revised continuously as conditions have seemed to demand, is still in operation.

Each comprehensive course was at first administered within the subject matter department most closely related to the general scope of the course and headed by a chairman of the course who in some cases was also the department head. Since the academic year 1952–1953, however, the comprehensive courses have been collected into a Department of General Studies. The head of this department is administratively coordinate with the heads of other departments of the college. Within the department each comprehensive course has its own chairman.

The Department of General Studies provides focus for the general education program on the Kansas State College campus and provides also the framework for expediting the course offerings. Whereas formerly all members of the faculty teaching comprehensive courses were members of subject matter departments and taught both general education courses and single field courses in regular departments, there are now a number of faculty members who teach full time in the Department of General Studies. This department, however, also continues to make use of faculty members from other subject matter departments on a shared or part-time basis. When his time is divided evenly between the two responsibilities, the faculty member is expected to choose membership with tenure in either the Department of General Studies or the subject matter department. When more than half time is devoted to a given department, the teacher holds permanent membership with tenure in that department. Staff members who teach in more than one department, however, have faculty privileges in both departments.

After emphasizing that "Not all of our problems have been completely solved by any means . . ." A. L. Pugsley, Dean of Academic Administration at Kansas State College, in a letter to the writer goes on to say, "By and large, however, I would say that we have made great progress."

University of Wisconsin. At the University of Wisconsin, the general education program is vested in the Department of Integrated Liberal Studies (ILS) which is an organic part of the College of Letters and Science. The program was put into operation in the fall of 1948.

At Wisconsin the general education program is optional and voluntary. It is a limited operation; not more than 300 new students may be admitted in any one fall term. Within the program the basic scheme of courses is required of all ILS students and is closed to others. This scheme facilitates total integration of materials presented and preserves the identity of the ILS group, thus fostering free discussion. Over and beyond the required ILS program, time is provided for elective courses elsewhere in the university.

It is a policy of the Department of Integrated Liberal Studies that each professor is free to plan his own course. Insofar as practicable, each course is taught by one person. Guest lecturers may be invited to participate in a given course, but always such participation is a contribution to the course as planned by the professor in charge.

Faculty members in the general education program at the University of Wisconsin are not separated from their academic department associations. All professors in the program are "borrowed" from other departments in the College of Letters and Science. According to Robert C. Pooley, Chairman of the Department of Integrated Liberal Studies, "This policy has permitted the recruitment of extremely able and prominent members of the faculty for ILS, and retaining them despite other calls on their time and energy." Apparently the ILS faculty has developed an extraordinary loyalty to the program. The program is now in its eleventh year of operation. Of the eighteen professors teaching in the program at present, ten have been continuously connected with ILS since its beginning; four others can claim five or more years of service.

The general education program at the University of Wisconsin is small in terms of numbers; it serves well, however, the students who participate in it.

University of Minnesota. At the University of Minnesota there are two completely separate programs of general education. The General College opened its doors in 1932. The general education program in the College of Science, Literature, and the Arts was started about ten years later. Only the program of the General College will be discussed here.

The General College at the University of Minnesota is designed to meet the academic needs of students who are not likely to remain in college more than one or two years. The only requirement for admission to the General College is graduation from high school. Admission to the other schools and colleges of the university is more selective.

In the General College the general education program is organized into seven major areas (not courses): (1) personal orientation, including individual and vocational orientation; (2) home life orientation; (3) social civic orientation; (4) general arts; (5) literature, speech, and writing; (6) biological science; and (7) physical science. In addition to the general education program, substantial sequences in vocational education are offered.

The program in the General College is not prescribed. No single course is required of all students. Rather, each student in consultation with his adviser elects his own program to meet his own particular needs.

A distinctive feature of the college is its student personnel program. Counseling, teaching, and administration work hand in hand. This "counseling point of view" pervades all of the activities of the college.

Another feature of the program in the General College is the single general comprehensive examination which covers all of the seven major areas of the general education curriculum noted earlier. One form of this examination is administered to the student upon his admission, a second form at the end of his first year of residence, and a third form when he completes his two years and his candidacy for the Associate of Arts degree. This examination is therefore invaluable to the adviser in helping the student to plan his program and to round out his general education. A definite level of achievement is specified on the final administration of the general comprehensive examination for candidacy for the two-year degree or for transfer to a four-year college.[1]

Administratively, the General College is a separate and independent instructional unit which has its own budget. Its dean reports directly to the president of the university. An assistant dean shares administrative responsibilities. For operational purposes, the college is organized into divisions.

The General College has its own carefully selected faculty. All levels of professional rank are open to staff members, each of whom also participates in the counseling program. On a part time basis there is some "trading" of faculty members with other instructional units of the university. Basically, however, the General College depends upon its own personnel resources in the operation of its program.

The General College has made numerous substantial and positive contributions to American higher education. Although it was set up as an experiment, it has demonstrated its value by fulfilling its objectives. It may now be considered to be a regular part of the organizational pattern of the University of Minnesota. Its future seems assured.

STATE COLLEGES AND STATE TEACHERS COLLEGES

State University of New York College for Teachers at Buffalo. The general education program in the College for Teachers in Buffalo is of fairly recent origin. Because it promises to become an effective program, it is considered here.

Buffalo can trace the beginning of its general education program to 1950. After much work a committee appointed by the president recommended six objectives for a proposed program and nine areas for courses to accomplish the objectives. The nine courses which eventuated are: (1) Man and His Institutions, (2) Mathematics and Modern Life, (3) Ways of Knowing, (4) Effective Communication, (5) Family Living, (6) Man and His Natural Environment, (7) The Arts of Living, (8) Ideas of Man and His World in Literature, and (9) Ideas and Social Change in Western Civilization. The first pilot sections of these courses were started in 1955. By June 1958, all of the courses had been taught in pilot section at least once. The program is now in the process of moving into full scale operation. This transition will require two years.

The general education courses are spread over the full four

years of college work. Most of the work is taken during the first two years. One course, however, is given in the junior year and one in the senior year. When the program gets into full operation two years hence, all students in the college during the regular academic year will be in at least one of the general education courses in any given term or enrollment period. Altogether, roughly one-quarter of the total effort of the college will be devoted to general education.

At the College for Teachers at Buffalo, general education is organized into a separate division whose director (first employed in 1956) has status, duties, and responsibilities coordinate with directors of the other curricular divisions. The division is organized into course staffs. Each general education course has its own chairman, a position which in status is roughly equal to a chairmanship in a traditional department in the Division of Arts and Sciences.

At the core of the general education staff are the full time members of the Division of General Education. In addition to the full time professional staff, many faculty members from other divisions of the college assist in the program, their contributions to general education ranging from one-fifth to four-fifths of their total time. Altogether, nearly one-third of the entire college staff is involved full time or part time in the general education program.

William D. Baker, Director of the Division of General Studies, summarizes his letter to the author in these words: "The major change that general education has brought about and will continue to bring about [in this institution] is the revolution in thinking about the aims of education and methods of teaching. This is true, I suspect, wherever general education programs are effective."

Colorado State College. For thirty years the Colorado State College has been studying and working with its general education program. The first courses in this program were offered in the fall of 1929.

At Colorado State forty-five quarter-hours of academic work

in general education are required. Basic courses are offered in five areas: natural sciences, social sciences, humanities, general psychology, and personal living. The first three of these courses represent the basic-fields approach to general education; the last two are modified forms of the student-needs approach. Through long experience, through study, and through evaluation these courses have, during the past three decades, evolved from survey or orientation courses into integrated courses which disregard departmentalized subject matter in order to maintain continuity and to treat knowledge in meaningful wholes.

The administration of the general education program at Colorado State College is decentralized. The college is organized into divisions and each division is responsible for the organization and administration of its courses in general education. The Curriculum Committee makes policy for the program. The Director of Instruction is responsible for the prevention of unnecessary duplication and overlapping of subject matter. A philosophy of general education is broadly accepted on the campus.

Colorado State has made much progress in its general education program during the past thirty years. But there is still more to do. In a letter to the writer, Donald G. Decker, Director of Instruction, states, "The greatest need is for the establishment of a single program rather than several divisional programs. The total program must take precedence over the desires of individual divisions."

Kansas State Teachers College. At the Kansas State Teachers College in Pittsburg, courses designed to meet needs in general education have been organized in the areas of communication, literature, fine arts, biology, physical science, mathematics, and social sciences. The minimum requirement is for thirty-six semester hours of work in these areas. For the most part, a single instructor teaches the entire course. Organizationally, there is no separate instructional staff for the general education program.

Teachers are not drafted into the general education program; they volunteer or enlist. This policy has resulted in the general education program having on its staff some of the best members of the entire faculty. The professional rewards for teaching in general education are at least equal to the professional rewards for other forms of service in the institution.

Kansas State Teachers College has no separate administrative organization for general education. The Dean of Instruction is in charge of academic functions of the entire college and he is vitally concerned with the general education program. The general courses are designed and offered by the regular departments of the college.

A feature of the general education program at Kansas State Teachers College is the Committee on General Studies. This committee is composed of all faculty members who teach one or more sections of the general courses. Heads of departments or divisions offering these courses, although they may not be teaching one of them, are *ex officio* members of the committee. The Dean of Instruction serves as chairman.

The Committee on General Studies is not an administrative body, but rather a deliberative one. In the committee, objectives and philosophy are discussed, course information is exchanged, ways of better correlating and integrating knowledge are sought, new developments in general education are considered, and new faculty members are indoctrinated and oriented into the program. The committee has played a leading role in advancing the goals of the general education program in this institution.

Ernest Mahan, Dean of Instruction, has long been associated with the general education program at Kansas State Teachers College. In a letter he writes, "In my judgment our organization and administration for general education, while accomplishing much, has fallen far short of what might have been accomplished under an improved organization. . . . Our College could take a giant step forward . . . if a separate Division of General Education could be created with its own chairman or dean and as far as feasible its own faculty. Much needed improvement in such areas as course design and instructional practices would come as a result."

Moorhead State College. Moorhead State College in Minnesota has built its program of general education about the following areas: communications, humanities, natural science, social studies, psychology of personal adjustment, and anthropology.

When the program of general studies was started, considerable attention was given to the administrative structure. Because of the relatively small size of the institution, a completely autonomous organization did not seem feasible. To place the general courses under the chairmen of the various departments and divisions also seemed questionable.

The solution was to create a Division of General Education and to establish a Council on General Education. The Division of General Education has academic status completely coordinate with all other divisions of the college. The Council on General Education operates as a part of the administrative organization in the same way other councils operate. It is made up of a representative of each of the areas of the program. The general policy is that chairmen of divisions and departments do not serve on the Council on General Education. This policy is intended to avoid any possibility of designing or using courses in general education to serve the interests of any particular area of specialization, or the introduction of activities and content materials aimed at recruitment for a particular division or department.

The Council on General Education, which has strong administrative support from the president of the institution, has complete authority to determine policies and to recommend changes in curriculum and requirements. For the most part, there has been close cooperation with other divisions in the selection of faculty that teach both general education and specialized courses.

At Moorhead State College the organizational structure here described has proved adequate through the years, and general education has become an accepted part of the academic program of the institution.

San Francisco State College. Under the leadership of former President J. Paul Leonard, the faculty of the San Francisco State College during the years 1946 and 1947 studied and planned a program of general education. Based on a representative sampling of students, an intensive and comprehensive study was made of student needs. The San Francisco community was studied in detail. General education programs in other institutions were investigated. Faculty conferences were held. The interest of the entire faculty was enlisted. As a result of this study and planning, the general education program was initiated in 1948. Continued interest on the part of the faculty has been in evidence ever since the program was started. The result has been constant review and assessment with consequent modification, growth, and improvement.

The general education program constitutes forty-five semester hours of course work—a little more than one-third of the total number of semester hours needed for the baccalaureate degree. The program is required. Entering freshmen must take all of the following courses, regardless of their vocational goals: Basic Communication; Personal, Social, and Occupational Development; The Contemporary Social World; The Development of American Institutions and Ideals; Contemporary Economic Society; International and Intercultural Relations; Human Biology and Health; The Physical World; Mathematics in Human Affairs; A Study of Values; Home and Family Living; Creative Arts Exploration; and Physical Education.

Although in the beginning there was some feeling that a separate division of general education ought to be established, the idea was rejected because it was felt that the general program should be the responsibility of the entire institution.

San Francisco State College is organized into eight administrative divisions, each headed by a chairman. The various courses in the general education program are assigned to the appropriate divisions. Within the division, each course has a coordinator other than, and in addition to, the division chairman. The line of administrative authority thus runs: president to dean of instruction to division chairman to general education course coordinator to general education course staff.

Policy matters follow another line of responsibility. The chief policy-making agency of the college is the Faculty Council. Reporting to the Faculty Council is the Instructional Policies Council, and reporting to the Instructional Policies Council is the Committee on General Education. The line of authority on policy matters follows: Faculty Council to Instructional Policies Council to Committee on General Education to division teaching staff to general education course teaching staff. These lines of responsibility seem rather cumbersome but apparently the scheme works effectively in this particular institution.

A word needs to be said about the Committee on General Education, the chief policy-making body of the college for the general education program. The committee is composed of one representative from each division, one from the AFROTC, and one from the student personnel staff, as well as the curriculum evaluator, the general education coordinator, and the Dean of Instruction, *ex officio*. This group oversees the entire general education program and formulates policy where and when such is indicated. The committee has the courses in the program under constant review. It encourages and facilitates integration among courses and course staffs and promotes the general development of the whole program. Any basic change in the program must be approved by this body.

Finally, mention should be made of two additional officers who assist in the operation of the program. The Coordinator of General Education was first appointed in 1956. He is a staff officer to the Dean of Instruction. He is in constant contact with the general education course coordinators, the general education course staffs, and the Committee on General Education of which he is an *ex officio* member. He is often given assignments not only by the Dean of Instruction but also by the Committee on General Education itself. He does whatever he can to facilitate and improve the operation of the general education program.

The Curriculum Evaluator, who also is an *ex officio* member of the Committee on General Education, likewise is a staff officer to the Dean of Instruction. He gives only a portion of his time to general education. His primary purpose is to help initiate self-appraisal programs and to aid individual instructors in their efforts to improve the effectiveness of their own courses. The Curriculum Evaluator is not an administrative officer, but rather serves the teaching divisions of the college and individual faculty members toward the ultimate goal of improvement of instruction.

In correspondence with the writer, Reginald Bell, Dean of Instruction, says of the general education program at San Francisco State College, "The present organization works very well. It probably is as efficient as any organizational structure and is certainly better for us than most alternative possibilities."

LIBERAL ARTS COLLEGES

Colgate University. The general education program at Colgate University dates from 1929. That year the faculty voted to introduce survey courses in five principal fields. During World War II, however, the program was completely restudied. As a result of this restudy and beginning in the fall of 1946 an essentially new program of general education, based largely on the use of problems and emphasizing good teaching, went into operation. Subsequent modifications have brought the program to its present form which extends through the full four years of baccalaureate work and includes the following courses: Problems in Physical Science, Problems in Biological Science, Problems in Philosophy and Religion, Problems in Music and the Visual Arts, Literature, Communication, Area Studies (one of several geographical areas of the world), American Ideals and Institutions (a junior course), and America in the World Community (a senior course).

Directly responsible for the general education program at Colgate is the Director of University Studies. This individual reports to the Dean of the Faculty and holds status equal to that held by the directors of the other divisions of the university. Each general education course has a director who, in responsibility and in time allowance for administration, is equivalent to a department chairman. The staff members for a particular general education course are drawn from the several departments which contribute to that course.

Each core course staff meets weekly for two hours or more to discuss both course content and procedures. In this way new colleagues are oriented and mutual education of the faculty across departmental lines is facilitated.

Although the Director of University Studies has no faculty of his own, he is consulted when new appointments are being considered in other divisions. Together with the directors of other divisions he advises the Dean of the Faculty concerning recommendations for salaries, tenure status, and promotions. This informal system works because of a common commitment to the general education program and a consequent attitude of cooperation toward it.

Herman A. Brautigam, Director of University Studies at Colgate, states in a letter to the writer, "The present organization and administration appear to be working well."

Chatham College. At Chatham College general education is conceived as an integral part of liberal education. The total program in this institution has been designed in such a way that general education and specialized training go hand in hand throughout the four years, with lessened emphasis each year on courses in general education and increased emphasis on specialized work.

The general education program at Chatham grew out of a long period of study on the part of the entire faculty. Even today the program has the flavor of belonging to the whole college.

Early in its deliberations the faculty came to an instrumental point of view—to a belief that the program of the college must be directed toward the preparation of students for real life situations. Knowledge is a means, not an end. The end of education is wisdom, a deep understanding of life, and an effective means of adjusting to it.

Beginning with this philosophical point of view the faculty in its early deliberations avoided discussions of courses, departments, requirements, and responsibility allocations. Instead it first concentrated upon the objectives of the program. Once the objectives took form and gained general acceptance, the faculty could then turn to the concrete problems of means and machinery. Throughout the process consideration was given not only to general education but also to other phases of a program of liberal education to make sure balance would result.

Out of these processes a general education program and general education courses evolved. The final result was a requirement extending through the full four years of college and involving a little more than half of the baccalaureate program. There are few institutions which have such heavy requirements in general education.

The program as it stands today involves work in the following areas: human development and behavior, The history of Western civilization, modern society, world issues, the arts, a course in a natural science (chemistry, biology, physics, or astronomy—preferably one which was not taken in secondary school), history and philosophy of science, English composition, effective speech, physical education, and philosophy of life.

The last-named course deserves further mention. This is a capstone, integrative course taken throughout the senior year. The objective of the course is to introduce the student to the world of values and to provide an opportunity for significant philosophical and religious thinking and discussion.

We have seen that general education at Chatham is an undertaking of the entire faculty. The administration of the program is relatively simple. The commitment of the president to the goals of general education is well known. Under him a dean of the college has over-all administrative responsibilities for the program. Each basic course has its own chairman since the courses are regarded as institutional rather than departmental in emphasis. Budgets for these courses are also independent of departmental budgets.

The policy-making body for the general education program is the Curriculum Committee. This committee consists of nine people, three elected each year for three-year terms. The committee has responsibility for all phases of the curriculum of the college, including the general education program. No essential change can be made in any phase of the program of general studies without the consent of this body.

Writing to the author of this chapter Paul R. Anderson, President, summarized his reactions to the Chatham program in these words: "The present organization is about as functionally effective as we can make it. . . . I can only say that our present system works."

Sarah Lawrence College. Like Chatham, Sarah Lawrence College does not draw a sharp line of demarcation between general and liberal education. Rather it conceives general education to be an integral part of liberal education; they are, in fact, two phases of the same educational entity. Also like Chatham College, Sarah Lawrence is committed to an instrumentalist philosophy of education. Its curriculum has been built on the principle that the individual student is the center of education.

In summarizing the program at Sarah Lawrence, the writer has chosen to quote at some length a letter from former President Harold Taylor.

> First a word about general education as a concept. We do not believe in the kind of general education which surveys given areas of the curriculum in an effort to achieve subject-matter coverage. We prefer to have students choose three areas, or courses, each year in terms of their own interests and the aims they have in mind for their college education. In each of the courses chosen, a student is encouraged to go deeply into a few topics rather than to spread widely over a given area in the subject. . . . In this sense, we do not belong in the general education movement since we try to have our students go deeply into a few areas rather than otherwise. In the sense that we do not believe in departmental course offerings or sequences of courses leading toward a major, we do belong in the general education movement, with the difference that we plan individually for each student rather than having a program for all.
>
> Since the beginning of the College we have had a system by which students choose three courses, each for a full year, and the program continues intact as of now. The content of the courses is determined individually by each teacher and usually changes from year to year as the teacher experiments with different methods and materials. In order that there will not be too much overlapping, a faculty-elected Committee on

Curricular Problems has final authority in determining what courses will be offered in a given year. An effort is made to match up the interests of the students with the interests of the faculty, so that the person teaching at Sarah Lawrence is teaching exactly what he cares about most to students who themselves are, by reason of their choice of the given area, interested in the things he has to teach . . .

Since there is essentially no demarcation between general education and liberal education at Sarah Lawrence and since the college is relatively small (some 400 students) administrative provisions are quite simple. Former President Taylor continues:

I think that the most effective part of our educational program is the freedom which each faculty member has to build his own courses as he sees fit. We have no formal departmental structure . . . philosophers, psychologists, religious thinkers, anthropologists, social scientists meet together in a group called social science, while others interested in philosophy, psychology, poetry, literary criticism, etc., meet together in the literature faculty. There are chairmen elected annually on a rotating basis, but the chairman has no power or authority. He simply acts as discussion leader for curricular talk . . .

St. John's College. Like Chatham and Sarah Lawrence, St. John's College in Annapolis does not distinguish between general education and liberal education. But there the likeness ends. St. John's is at the other end of the philosophical spectrum. It is committed to the philosophy of rationalism, a neo-Thomistic philosophy which advances the belief that within the work of the classical writers may be found basic principles and absolute values which reveal the basic nature of the universe and the relation of man to nature and God. The proper orientation of general education, therefore, lies in a serious study of the past.

St. John's offers a single required course built around a study of the great books of our Western tradition. During the four years leading to the bachelor's degree, approximately one-hundred of these great books are read and digested. The program operates around semi-weekly laboratories in the natural sciences, and a formal lecture each week.

St. John's is a small college (about 200 students) with a small faculty. Administratively, its problems are simple. There are no departments, only one faculty. Nor does the faculty have rank; all except the teaching interns (who are graduate students) are simply designated as tutors. Within this administrative framework general education and liberal education alike operate as integral parts of the total program.

Different though the program at St. John's is from general education programs offered in other American colleges and universities, in the philosophical framework within which it operates it must be described as effective.

JUNIOR COLLEGES

Contra Costa Junior College District. The Contra Costa Junior College District in California operates two junior colleges: Diablo Valley College and Contra Costa College. Each college is headed by a director. Reporting to each director are two deans: a Dean of Instruction and a Dean of Student Personnel. The duties and responsibilities of these respective deans are adequately described by their titles. Each Dean of Instruction has an Advisory Committee on Instruction composed of faculty members from representative areas of his college. There is no departmental or divisional organization with the colleges.

In each of the two colleges the administration of the general education program is the responsibility of the Dean of Instruction. It follows that before appointment to this position the candidate is carefully investigated concerning his educational philosophy and his commitment to general education.

In Diablo Valley College and Contra Costa College a substantial portion of the junior college program, whether it be terminal or transfer, is in the field of general education. Graduation requirements assure this.

In these two colleges, general education is considered the responsibility of all faculty members, not only those designated to teach the courses organized for this purpose. The organization of the total instructional program under one person (the Dean of Instruction, who is consulted by the Advisory Committee on

Instruction), coupled with the absence of departments and divisions, not only implements the philosophy of faculty-wide participation but also adequately places responsibility with one person who has the overall authority to make the philosophy effective. It is felt that the most effective way of enhancing the general education programs in the colleges is to employ only faculty members who, regardless of their teaching fields, are deeply committed to a general-education point of view. Within this overlying philosophy and within this administrative framework, the colleges have been successful in getting staff agreement on the objectives of general education and in enlisting effective staff effort in the operation of the general education program.

Orange Coast College. In each of its two-year programs Orange Coast College, one of California's public junior colleges, requires a substantial amount of general education. The general courses required of all students include the following: Introductory Psychology, Communication Skills, Health Education, Physical Education, and American History and Institutions. In addition, students are urged to elect from the following courses which have been designed to make significant contributions to general education: Life Science, Physical Science, Consumer Economics, Fundamentals of Living, American Literature, History and Appreciation of Music, Introduction to Art, Marriage and Family Life, Group Dynamics, Industrial Relations, Applied Mathematics, Business Mathematics, and Mathematics for Industry.

Because of its relatively modest size (about 1,500 daytime students) and the overall character of its program, the administrative structure is not complicated. Much of the developmental work is handled directly by the entire faculty rather than through committees. This direct involvement, coupled with the fact that all faculty members are employed at least in part because of their commitment to a belief in this kind of education, lends an institution-wide character to the general education program at Orange Coast College. Furthermore, a continuous program of in-service training enhances a feeling of unity among faculty members and keeps them alert to problems and developments in general education.

At Orange Coast the Curriculum Committee serves also as the Committee on General Education. This committee is composed of two administrators, the seven division chairmen, and representatives of the faculty; it operates under the chairmanship of the vice president of the college. As the chief policy-making body for the general education program it keeps the program under constant review, passes on all proposals concerning the program, recommends and supervises studies, and continually evaluates the program.

Concerning the general education program at Orange Coast College, President Basil H. Peterson writes to the author of this chapter, "We feel that it operates quite satisfactorily."

Stephens College. Stephens College offers a program of functional general education for women, a program which holds the needs of the individual student to be of paramount importance. The program has grown out of research and experimentation which started in 1921 and which has continued to the present. In the general education scheme the position of religion is central. Group living and extracurricular activities are considered integral parts of the general education program. The whole intricate undertaking is made to work through an excellent system of counseling.

Early research by the late W. W. Charters and further study by the faculty revealed that all women—married or single, employed in the home or outside the home—perform activities and have problems in the following areas: (1) communications, (2) appreciation of the beautiful, (3) social adjustment, (4) physical health, (5) mental health, (6) consumer problems, (7) philosophy of life, (8) knowledge and understanding of the world of science, (9) home and family relations, and (10) occupational planning. The general education program at Stephens is designed to deal with these activities and problems. Numerous courses have been developed to facilitate the operation of the program, yet there is no required course in the program. Through guidance and counseling the work is tailored to each individual student.

The general education program at Stephens operates within a surprisingly simple and flexible administrative structure. The program is characterized by efficient administration through close cooperation among the president, the vice president, the deans, and the division heads. Channels are open from the faculty to all administrative officers, including the president.

The president of the college appoints the Vice President for Academic Affairs (who also serves as Dean of Instruction), the Dean of Religious Life, the Dean of Students, and the Director of Research. These four officers work directly with the president as consultants and advisors.

Under the Vice President for Academic Affairs, the college is organized into eight divisions, each of which has its own division head. The divisions offer both basic courses in general education and specialized courses of a traditional nature. Both kinds of courses are taught by staff members drawn from within the division.

A feature of the Stephens program is that every faculty member also serves as a faculty adviser and counselor. Difficult problems are referred to specialists whose services are always available at the college.

Within this flexible and adaptable organization the general education program at Stephens College works. According to the Vice President for Academic Affairs, James G. Rice:

> My feeling is that our present organization and administration is as good as any which I can conceive. The prerequisites for operating a program of general education seem to me to depend upon the building of a faculty and staff dedicated to an education which produces changes in students and upon communication and understanding among these people as they work together toward this end. No doubt there are some organizations which work better as organizations than others, but the kind of mind which places emphasis on categories, lines of authority, and parliamentary procedure does not seem to me to be the kind of mind

which will, in the end, develop a worthwhile program of general education.

Chicago City Junior College. The Chicago City Junior College, an institution now having six branches and serving well over 16,000 students, has offered a program of general education continuously since 1934. All two-year curricula include prescribed courses in English (communications), biology, humanities, physical science, social science, and physical education. These courses constitute the basic curriculum, and are designed to introduce the student to the principal fields of knowledge and to provide the breadth of training desirable in a well-rounded education.

Although the General Superintendent of Schools in Chicago is also president of the college, the chief administrator of the academic program is the Dean of the Chicago City Junior College. He has direct responsibility for all six branches. In addition each branch has an assistant dean in charge.

Within each of the branches of the Chicago City Junior College a number of departments (actually divisions in a number of cases) have been established. In some instances local and personnel factors rather than logic determined the number and scope of departments.

In the operation of the general education program departmental lines are abolished. Traditional departmental barriers cease to exist and a satisfactory degree of integration is achieved. Perhaps this cooperation between and among departments can be explained because CCJC is a two-year institution; vested interests are probably not deeply ingrained. Experience shows that in four-year institutions departmental loyalties are usually quite deep rooted.

New teachers in the general education program have, as far as possible, been trained in the newer, broader areas of knowledge. In-service training is in continuous process in the general education courses for both new and old faculty members.

In a memorandum to the author, Peter Masiko, Jr., Dean of the Chicago City Junior College, writes, "In general, we are satisfied with the organization and administration of our general education program."

PRINCIPLES OF EFFECTIVE ADMINISTRATION

The administrative structures and practices of more than a score of institutions operating effective general education programs have been described. No two are entirely alike. In some institutions the organizational and administrative provisions for the general education program are complex; in others they are quite simple. Some programs operate within independent organizational structures; in others there is no special organizational machinery and the general education program operates as an integral part of the total program of the institution. Some general education programs have special officers to administer them; others are handled by the regular and traditional officers of the institution. Some general education programs are staffed by specially selected faculty members who teach nothing but general courses; others are taught effectively by instructors who offer work both in general education and in their fields of specialization; still others, unfortunately, are taught by people who have little or no sympathy for general education and ought not to be in the program. Some general education programs have their own budgets; others do not. In operating its general education program, each institution has moved forward in its own way. Diversity, not uniformity, characterizes the organization and administration of general education as it does all of American higher education.

Out of this diversity of approaches, however, emerge certain principles of organization and administration which an institution contemplating the establishment of a general education program would do well to consider:

1. *The inauguration of a program of general education should begin with an analysis of the particular student body and the results to be achieved with these students.* Student bodies differ in abilities, interests, and needs. The general education program ought to be based on these differences. A general education

program which will work effectively in one institution may be completely inappropriate in another.

2. *To insure success, wide use of the faculty in planning the general education program is essential.* A rationale must be developed, a philosophy must be adopted, objectives must be established, and courses and programs must be planned. This planning should involve the whole faculty, not only those who will teach the general education courses.

3. *Strong administrative support is indispensable.* Without strong administrative support, an effective program of general education is impossible; without this support such a program should never be attempted. Among other things the administration should let it be known that it regards general education to be important to the extent that salaries, promotions, and other factors of professional advancement in this program are equal to those otherwise operating within the institution.

4. *The general education program should be designed to meet the needs of the specific institution.* Size, composition of student body, faculty, physical resources, philosophical orientation, course offerings, institutional organization, and other factors will all enter into this design. It is a mistake for one institution to adopt *in toto* the general education program of another institution. In order to be successful, these programs must fit the needs of the particular institutions in which they operate.

5. *Responsibility for leadership and coordination of the general education program should be placed within one office.* This responsibility may be allocated to an individual or a committee. While cooperation is a *sine qua non* of general education planning and functioning, it is a fundamental principle of organization and administration that the entire operation of a program of this kind must head up in a single person or agency.

6. *Except possibly in small institutions it is unwise to permit general education courses to be administered by department heads.* It is difficult for one person to administer two different kinds of programs and to give equal support to both. Since specialization has traditional status, it is easy to continue to view it

with favor and to question another type of program which in many colleges and universities must still be regarded as experimental. General education courses belong to the whole institution, not to departments.

7. *The content of general education courses should be instrumental rather than encyclopedic in character.* These courses should function effectively in the lives of students. There seems little doubt that general education in America is moving toward a philosophy of instrumentalism.

8. *In an effective program of general education good teaching must be regarded as critically important.* Changes in curriculum will not automatically improve instruction. If the teacher of general courses does not accept them with enthusiasm and with belief in their worth, his teaching will likely be spiritless, aimless, and ineffective. Without good teaching the whole enterprise fails.

9. *Students should be given adequate orientation to the general education program as a whole.* General education may be new to some students and its purposes may not be understood. Once adequately explained, however, the program will make sense to students; they will almost invariably accept it as a good thing. To accomplish this understanding appropriate orientation is required.

10. *Opportunity should be given students to earn credit and/or exemption from general education requirements by examination.* This policy recognizes intellectual growth and academic achievement by means other than college courses. Superior students who can demonstrate understanding at acceptable levels of excellence should be excused, with or without credit, from further required work in general education. The awarding of credit and/or exemption by examination is a waxing practice in American higher education.

11. *Adequate counseling is an absolute requirement in an effective program of general education.* College work and college living are complex undertakings. Only through adequate counseling can students hope to deal with them effectively.

12. *A program of evaluation at a professional level should*

constitute an integral part of the general education program. Evaluation not only helps the student estimate his growth; it also helps faculty members develop insights into the nature of students, clarify the objectives of general education, appraise student progress, and improve methods of teaching. In general education, good instruction and effective evaluation go hand in hand as inseparable—almost indistinguishable—partners.

13. *The general education program should be conceived and developed as an entity—not as a series of disparate courses, isolated odds and ends, or disarticulated and uncoordinated educational activities and experiments.* There should be a wholeness within the general education program; the student who completes it should sense the satisfaction of having completed a meaningful and integrated educational experience.

NOTES

[1] *General Education in a Free Society,* Cambridge, Harvard University Press, 1945.

[2] The great majority of General College students do not progress beyond two years of college and it is for them that the program is intended. Some students, however, are awakened to a new interest and a new motivation and do acceptable "standard" college work. About one out of five General College students will accumulate an academic record (a "B" average) which will permit him to transfer to another school or college within the University of Minnesota and actually complete a four-year program.

Chapter III

CURRICULAR PROGRAMS IN GENERAL EDUCATION

RUSSELL M. COOPER
Dean, College of Liberal Arts,
University of South Florida

THE dynamics of the general educational movement rise from many sources—both within and outside the student and within and outside the college. As noted in Chapter I, there are widely varying curricular programs in America that are labeled with the term, general education. While different in philosophy and content, these programs yet have much in common, particularly in the purpose that impels them. For they all represent an earnest endeavor to meet a growing problem in modern society and in the collegiate community. Their ends are essentially the same even though their means may vastly differ.

The impulse behind general education arises from the condition of our time. It is a paradox that in an age when more people are proceeding with their education to a higher level than ever before there is still widespread confusion and frustration. The cultural lag between the onrush of technological progress and the capacity of men to understand their world and control it grows ever more ominous and threatens complete disaster. Society is plagued by recurring suicidal wars, economic booms and depressions, racial and national hostility, drunkenness and marital discord. Yet despite this challenge the cultural interests and habits of college graduates are often little different from those who never matriculated.

The persistence of such social and personal inadequacies has caused thoughtful persons to take a second look at the colleges and ask what has happened. Examination reveals that the colleges are embarrassed with a plethora of riches. The vast expansion of knowledge in all fields has made its full comprehension impossible. With the multiplication of hundreds—even thousands—of courses, no student can take more than a tiny fraction of the offerings available. He can pursue a highly technical curriculum for the full four years without either exhausting it or tasting the humanities. In the traditional liberal arts college he may find dozens of offerings quite unrelated to one another and only incidentally relevant to the problems of our current social and personal condition. Under such circumstances, it is a wise student indeed who can achieve a rounded and balanced view of life. He may easily run aground on the Scylla of overspecialization or the Charybdis of scattered, unrelated election.

The answer to this educational dilemma must obviously lie within education itself. And "general education" is a term applied to programs that are rising in response to the need. Such programs all seek to identity among the vast ranges of human knowledge those *fundamentals* essential to the well being of cultivated men. These essential ideas and intellectual skills must then be brought together in systematic and intelligible fashion in order that the student will be motivated to comprehend them and to apply them in his personal living.

General education is thus "general" in a number of ways. It is designed for *all* people irrespective of prospective vocation. It draws its material from *all* the academic disciplines, wherever basic and relevant ideas can be found. It is concerned with the student's *total* development, his values and aesthetic sensitivity as well as his purely intellectual attributes, for all these affect his comprehension and mature response to the world around him.

All programs of general education recognize that they are at once terminal and preparatory. Because the time which a student may divert from specialized education tends to be limited, he often takes only one or two courses in each broad field of subject matter, and for many students these may end formal instruction in that field. In any case, the general education course must be independent and significant in itself, not merely preparatory to a sequence of courses coming later. While collegiate general education courses are thus "terminal" in nature, they are expected also to excite student interest and promote habits of independent reading that will continue throughout life. Ideally, general education never ceases, but through many channels continues to give sparkle and understanding to man as a responsible human being and citizen.

The task undertaken by general education is formidable and shows no sign of diminution. Social problems become increasingly pressing and the explosion of knowledge with consequent curricular proliferation continues. The need for programs which can sift and integrate and interpret becomes daily more urgent.

One can scarcely question, therefore, the need for general education in our colleges. The real issue is concerned with the rationale and character of the program, and at this point practitioners in the movement have differed sharply. Such disagreement undoubtedly has often been healthy, for it has led to a wide variety of experimentation. It is too early to predict what the "best program" of general education may be like, and indeed with a constantly changing society and body of knowledge there can never be a final answer to this question. The superior programs will constantly be undergoing revisions to avoid obsolescence. But from the hundreds of courses with which college faculties have experimented during the past forty years, one can discern several types. It is important to look at each of these types carefully.

VARYING APPROACHES TO GENERAL EDUCATION

Distributive Requirements. The first venture of a faculty in meeting general education objectives is usually the establishment of distributive requirements. Nearly all colleges in America have now formulated rules to require that students spread their work among several different fields. Usually these regulations require a year's course or two in the social sciences, one or two years in the natural sciences, probably some work in foreign language or literature, and often a course or two in mathematics, English composition, physical education, and perhaps religion. In some cases specific courses are prescribed but often the student is given a choice among elementary courses offered by departments in the appropriate field.

This arrangement has had distinct advantages over a system of free election which might permit a student to concentrate all of his work in one or two departments. It has helped assure the balanced educational experience so necessary for a liberal education.

Moreover, a system of distributive requirements has been relatively easy to establish. No new courses are required since the student is asked simply to elect one of the existing introductory courses in an appropriate department. It usually commends itself to the faculty because every department (certainly the older and politically stronger ones) will be included in the new arrangement and will have an equal chance to attract students into its elementary courses. Where disagreements have arisen they have usually been over problems of classification, such as whether history should help satisfy the social science or the humanities requirement, whether or not mathematics should be considered a natural science, and how one should classify such departments as speech, home economics, psychology, and physical education. Such difficulties have usually been resolved in time and the distributive principle has become a nearly universal feature of American graduation requirements.

However, the distributive regulations fall so far short of meeting general education needs that many persons would not even consider them part of the general education movement. Perhaps the most serious limitation lies in the great gaps that are still permitted in the student's education. If the natural science requirement can be met by an elementary course in physics or in chemistry or in geology or in astronomy, he will have some background in that field but be largely ignorant of the others (except perhaps as his high school background may help fill the gaps). Yet a citizen should today have some acquaintance with the general principles and vocabulary basic to all the sciences if he is to become part of an informed public and join with others in making policy decisions concerning scientific matters. The same problem arises for a student who takes a course in economics, but has no sociology, political science, history, geography, or anthropology, hence being able to examine only one facet of a social problem rather than perceiving its interdisciplinary complexity.

Defenders of the distribution principle for meeting general education needs will often contend that concentration upon a single department or course will give the student a penetration into the field and a method of analysis which will be more substantial than in any alternative program, and that such intellectual faculties can then be used for attacking the problems of related fields whenever occasions arise. They will argue also that if the introductory course is well taught, the instructor will find many opportunities for pointing out relations to other fields of thought and hence it becomes somewhat interdisciplinary.

There is of course some merit in these contentions, though in most cases they must be heavily discounted. It is doubtful whether a single freshman course in a science department, even with laboratory included, gives a student such a grasp of scientific method that he can use it for solving problems arising in other fields, particularly when he has no factual background in those fields. Systematic thinking on any problem is practically impossible without the essential elements of information in mind or at hand. Likewise, it is doubtful whether a resourceful economics professor will discuss the sociological, political, and other aspects of a problem as thoroughly as the economic factors; and to the extent that he does take time to do this he cannot meet departmental expectations for preparing students for advanced work in the economic fields.

This last point leads directly to another serious charge against programs which rely on the distributive system. Introductory courses are usually designed not for the general student but for the few who are going on to major in that field. Such courses may become at once too technical and too elementary for the general student. For example, the musically inclined student meeting his science requirement by the elementary course in chemistry will normally take a year of inorganic chemistry, entailing more mathematical precision and memorization of technical terminology than he needs for his purposes. On the other hand, information about organic compounds and other major chemical ideas important to the layman are completely denied him. They do not come until the second year.

Besides these two charges against the distribution system, that of one-sidedness and of irrelevance, there is the further consideration that such courses often are so preoccupied in laying a factual foundation for pre-majors that there is little or no time to explore the philosophical, historical, and humane elements of the field which are of greatest interest and importance to the general student. Those may well be the elements which will excite his intellectual curiosity and encourage him to go on with serious reading long after he has finished college. But if his contact with the field is confined simply to the brick and mortar of factual memorization without opportunity to see the larger structure of meaning for human experience, an educational opportunity of great significance may be lost. And widespread testimony from the 50 per cent who drop out of college in mid stream—good students as well as bad—indicates that for many their education was a chore and a bore rather than an exciting intellectual quest. If, however, a student's general education course is something other than an elementary departmental course, the professor is under no compulsion to prepare him for advanced work and can range widely in selecting those elements of information, those basic principles and seminal ideas, which should stir even the uninitiated student to eagerness for more learning.

While it is recognized that introductory departmental courses can be used to assure a spread of work, and while in some departments such as history, English, and sociology such courses have often been directed to the interests of the general student, the distribution system nevertheless leaves so many problems unsolved that most proponents of general education have insisted on going further. They normally have kept the distribution requirements in some form but have demanded new courses explicitly designed for the general student, rather than the pre-major, as a means of satisfying these requirements. The character of such courses is discussed in the sections that follow.

Survey Courses. The first and obvious impulse of those who decry the traditionally narrow compartmentalization of the distribution system is to devise courses crossing a number of fields. Thus, instead of limiting the general student to a single course in economics or sociology, the new survey course may strive to summarize the essential principles of economics, sociology, political science, and geography in the course of the year's study. It is argued that by offering three or four broad survey courses, it may be possible to cover virtually all the basic fields of knowledge, thus providing a truly inclusive and rounded view of the world instead of three or four limited departmental views.

An early pioneer in this type of offering was a course organized at the University of Chicago in the mid-twenties under the leadership of a biologist, Professor Horatio H. Newman. The textbook prepared by Professor Newman and his colleagues was published by the University of Chicago Press in 1926 under the ambitious title: *The Nature of the World and of Man*. It sought to summarize fundamental information from astronomy, geology, physics, chemistry, botany, bacteriology, zoology, physical anthropology, human physiology, and psychology. In similar fashion there was organized at Dartmouth a few years later a course in the social sciences, giving rise to a two volume work by Riegel *et al.* called *An Introduction to the Social Sciences* and surveying essential principles from economics, government, and sociology. Colgate University pioneered with a similar series of five survey courses during the 1930's and the idea spread rapidly throughout the country.

While the earlier courses have almost entirely disappeared, they did yield some advantages and in modified form persist to the present day. They not only gave the student a broader background with which to continue his informal reading but they also acquainted him with a number of disciplines, thus helping him to choose a major. The courses were freed from the responsibility of preparing students for a hierarchy of sequence offerings and hence could select material freely on the basis of the general student's interest and need. Moreover, especially in their early stages, the surveys were rather easily organized administratively, for a member from each related department could be enlisted to give the lectures appropriate to this field. Qualified teachers were, therefore, immediately at hand.

But the survey course was found also to have serious limitations. For one thing, it proved impossible truly to "survey" the principles of any discipline in a few weeks' time, and the attempt resulted in such a high level of abstraction that the material often had little concrete meaning and applicability to the student. Subsequent development of the survey courses has made them more selective in nature, emphasizing only those points of greatest significance and leaving vast areas of the discipline entirely untouched. By this device, sometimes called the "block and gap system," one can teach a block of material with as much depth and concreteness as can be found in any elementary departmental course and yet sample several departmental fields in the course of the year. Courses given in this selective fashion, particularly in the natural sciences, have proved quite successful and are still widely taught.

A second difficulty with the survey course has arisen when many lecturers were collaborating, as many as sixteen in Professor Newman's course at Chicago. It is difficult to combine the work of all participants into an integrated whole, as each man tends to teach his own specialty in his own way. Not only is the student forced to adjust continually to new instructors with new approaches and expectations, but the overall meaning and interrelationships of the bits of knowledge seldom emerge. Even when a hard driving course chairman through many staff meetings has effected some continuity and unity in the course, the shifting personnel from year to year has made the maintenance of such unity difficult.

A further charge against the survey course has been that it tends to depict the organization of knowledge as systematically developed by the traditional disciplines, an organization of great value to the scholar but often having limited value to the general student. It may be more important for the student, for example, to study social phenomena as they practically arise in the community rather than to study the theoretical framework for analysis of such phenomena as devised within the disciplines. Again, therefore, the problem of relevance to student need becomes a major object of concern.

Where they have persisted, the survey courses have not only been rigorously selective in nature but have also usually been taught by a single professor who explores fundamental principles with the students and seeks continually to show interrelationships and applications to everyday life.

A variant from the survey of disciplines is the survey of topics or problems. Such courses have been particularly popular in the social sciences. For example, Atteberry, Auble, and Hunt developed a course of this kind in the Chicago Junior Colleges in the late 1930's and published a two-volume textbook called *Introduction to Social Science: A Survey of Social Problems* wherein each of the forty-nine chapters was devoted to a different social problem. These ranged from housing to the business cycle to American foreign policy. Presumably a class would spend a few days a week on each problem, examining relevant data from sociology, economics, government, or other sources which would clarify its character and importance in the larger social scene. Such courses can not hope to solve the problems discussed but rather are intended to introduce students to the complexities of the issues and help them examine divergent viewpoints and sources of data. These courses have been quite popular with students because they are down to earth, dealing with problems that they read about daily in the newspapers, and calling upon theoretical materials only as needed to illuminate the issue. While these courses also have been open to the charge of superficiality, they nevertheless seem to have served a useful purpose in stimulating the interest of students, giving them increased acquaintance with contemporary life and motivating them to further study.

In addition to interdisciplinary survey courses there have long been survey courses within the several disciplines. It has been common practice to offer a survey of Western philosophy from Thales to Whitehead, surveys of English literature from Beowulf to Virginia Woolf, surveys of European history from the fall of Rome to the fall of Hitler. Such surveys are common as introductory courses in many fields and have served a valuable orientation purpose though they are subject to the same criticism of superficiality that is often leveled against interdisciplinary surveys and they lack the compensatory virtue of giving the general student perspective over a broad division of subject matter. They are frequently found among the elementary departmental courses available to satisfy distributive requirements, as discussed in the previous section.

Great Books Courses. Courses in the "great books" have been popularized through such advocates as Robert Hutchins, Mortimer Adler, and the Great Books Foundation. The best prototype is to be found at St. John's College in Annapolis, Maryland, which is described in Chapter II.

At first glance it might seem that these courses are essentially surveys of the literature of the Western world and in a limited sense this is true. But actually the rationale behind the courses is very different from that of a typical survey course. The difference is so fundamental that it strikes at the nature of education and the learning process itself. Survey courses, like most introductory departmental courses, conceive of the mind as a reservoir which should be filled with as much knowledge as possible, knowledge which can subsequently be recalled for application as the occasion demands. The great books advocates, on the other hand, argue that the mind is not a reservoir to be filled with facts; in any case such facts will soon leak away or become obsolete. Rather the mind should be regarded as a tool, an instrument which when sharpened against the hard tough reasoning of the great minds of the ages will itself be able to cut through the sophistries and illogicalities of much modern thought. Because of this emphasis upon reason as the aim of education, such advocates are often referred to as rationalists, being thus distinguished from the neo-humanists who tend to be identified with survey courses.

Without question some of the great books enthusiasts have made an important contribution to contemporary culture. Through the courses offered at St. John's and more limitedly in many other institutions, and particularly through the adult discussion groups sponsored by The Great Books Foundation, tens of thousands of persons have discovered the excitement of reading provocative books in the original instead of stale, pre-digested summaries in textbooks. They have enjoyed the exhilaration of participating in the "great conversation" of thoughtful people down through the ages who have addressed themselves to fundamental issues of life.

On the other hand, the great books plan has serious limitations as a program of general education. For one thing it tends to ignore the enormous contributions of recent research to the problems under discussion, leaving the student almost nonconversant with the realities of modern science and social organization. Moreover, the plan rests upon a very dubious psychological principle of transfer. It assumes that if the mind is sharpened through the great books (and, as at St. John's, through extended study of mathematics and language) it will then be able to attack any modern issue with acuity. But psychological research demonstrates that such transfer is limited and tends to occur only when explicitly pointed out at the time of learning and even then only to problems of a similar character. Normally, the great books teachers make little effort to show contemporary applications of the material learned. In their writing they have often deplored such practical applications, as well as comments about the book's social setting or the author's background, as being a subversion of the main purpose.

Great books courses also have disadvantages as the preponderant program for freshmen. The typical student just out of high school is caught up in the interests and values of his peer culture and often he feels the great books to be irrelevant to his interests and difficult to comprehend. Mortimer Adler, one of the most enthusiastic advocates of the system, has recommended that the program not be offered to undergraduates but rather to the adult population who through special evening discussion groups can bring maturity and special understanding to the reading. For undergraduates, it would seem that great books can and should be read but in a different context from that discussed here, perhaps the context of the following two sections.

Problem Solving Courses.—A number of general education courses are built on the principle that students learn best when given a practical problem from contemporary life to analyze and resolve. The new natural science course at Colgate University, for example, poses seven problems, such as the origin of the Carolina Bays, forcing the student to read widely in several fields to gather the information which will help him to interpret the phenomena. The course in human relations at Harvard University is built on the case method whereby certain problems of man's experience are posed in graphic detail after which the student must read widely to find the data and principles to be applied. Ultimately the student is expected to weigh alternative solutions and arrive at one which he will espouse and defend. At Bennington College, and particularly at Sarah Lawrence, the entire curriculum is related to the student's special interests and needs, with a continuous challenge to tackle those studies and analyze those problems which thereby will help satisfy such needs.

This instrumentalist approach to general education has some of the premises of the great books approach since it also is concerned with training the mind to solve problems rather than filling the mind with carefully selected information from the cultural tradition. But the instrumentalist tackles the problem very differently from the rationalist. He insists that if the mind is to learn how to solve problems, it must do so by tackling independently and decisively the pressing issues at hand rather than by simply reading what ancient philosophers had to say about the matter. If one wishes to be an intellectual pioneer, he must learn how to blaze new thought trails for himself instead of following the well-trod paths of his forefathers.

In developing its courses, the instrumentalist school has been particularly influenced by the analyses of student needs worked out during the 1940's. *A Design for General Education* was published by the American Council on Education in 1944 to help structure courses meeting the general needs of servicemen. In 1947, the President's Commission on Higher Education issued a report citing eleven similar needs faced by all American youth. These included the development of personal ethical principles, preparation for citizenship, relation to world peace, understanding of the natural world, effective communication, satisfactory emotional adjustment, health, enjoyment of the arts, preparation for family life, vocational choice, and critical thinking. While all general education programs seek to serve these needs in some measure, those consciously focused upon the student naturally emphasize them the most.

Advocates of the problem solving method contend that their students are highly motivated because of the practicality and relevance of the problems under discussion. Moreover they argue that the emphasis upon independent thought and research tends to develop maturity and self-reliance on the part of the student. And in addition, through his pursuit of background materials, he may read more extensively and purposefully than will students under any other method. He may indeed read much material from the ancient philosophers but he does so with a self-imposed purpose and can be expected therefore to derive greater value.

Critics of this plan point out, however, that there is no assurance that the student will sample the many aspects of knowledge in systematic and well rounded fashion. He may pursue one rather narrow interest disproportionately or he may dabble here and there in various fields in his search for knowledge and fail to gain the intellectual perspective and poise available through more comprehensive approaches. Some have charged also that the method tends to make the student self-centered in his interests rather than an objective observer of life, though the record of students in institutions where the method prevails somewhat belies this charge. Advocates of the idea point out that in so far as transfer is feasible, it can be most readily expected from the problem solving method since the problems chosen are closely related to the realities of everyday experience which the student will continue to explore after graduation.

Great Issues Courses. Courses in "great issues" or "big ideas" have been popularized by the well known senior course at Dartmouth, but actually their origin goes back much earlier. The grandfather of the modern general education movement, the Contemporary Civilization course inaugurated by John Erskine and his colleagues at Columbia University in 1919, should probably be classified in this group. The Columbia course, which has continued as a required offering to the present day, sought to acquaint the student with the major intellectual foundations of contemporary society, enabling him to understand the underlying issues of the current political and ideological struggle.

While such courses have been developed in the sciences, for example Harvard's Historical Introduction to the Physical Sciences, they are much more common in the social sciences and humanities. In the social sciences, the endeavor is to deal not only with manifest social problems but more particularly with the struggles and processes which give rise to such problems. The courses deal with the effort of the individual personality to find meaning and satisfaction in the larger social group. They are concerned with political, economic, and social institutions and their tendency toward centralization and bureaucracy. They may examine the interaction of community and technology. In analyzing such questions, materials are drawn from all the social sciences and the emergent manifestations in current political life are scrutinized. But the chief purpose is to help the student perceive the underlying realities and dynamics of the social process.

In the humanities, these courses are concerned with such issues as the problem of good and evil, the nature of man as related to the cosmos, the cultural impact of such figures as Darwin, Marx, and Freud, and the common elements among the fine arts. Again, the student is brought to probe beneath the surface of everyday experience to see the intellectual and spiritual struggles that underlie it.

While these courses have something in common with those mentioned in the sections above, it will be seen that they are really quite different in spirit and purpose. Materials root back into the cultural tradition but there is no attempt to explore them in the systematic manner of the several disciplines as is done in survey courses. Students in these great issues classes likewise read many of the great books in their entirety. But they study such books not because they are "great" for disciplining and sharpening the mind, but rather because they have something important to say about the problem under discussion. Many of the readings may not even be great literary or philosophical masterpieces, but are chosen because they expound a divergent view or otherwise illuminate the problem provocatively and precisely.

These great issues courses are akin to the instrumentalist approach in that they are built around significant problems, but the endeavor is more to illuminate a problem than to solve it. There is usually less emphasis upon the student's independent exploration of related fields and more upon commonality of class experience. The mind is conceived not as a reservoir to store essential facts nor as a knife to be sharpened but rather as a lens to be polished in order that the realities of life may be observed more clearly and its beauties apprehended more sensitively.

Advocates of this kind of course contend that it is a good vehicle for motivating student interest because the problems are significant and relevant to everyday experience and excellent readings can readily be found. Ordinarily, both the topics and the readings are new to the undergraduate student, seldom duplicated in high school and often nowhere else in college. The student is made to feel a part of his culture and to develop the language and concerns of cultivated men. He starts the habit of reading good books in their entirety and coming to terms with the authors, and he develops a hunger for more such reading in the future.

While these are impressive advantages, it must be recognized that the system lacks some of the values found in other types of courses. For example, the student does not necessarily achieve a chronological perspective of the development of our Western tradition nor any systematic understanding of the organization of the several disciplines. Those values may be better found in the survey courses. Usually the materials read are of a literary or philosophical rather than empirical nature, and in the social sciences the student may be left with an inadequate awareness of the methodology of current social scientific research. The courses, as usually taught, involve considerable class discussion and encouragement to independent reflection, and yet they tend to maintain the traditional academic lockstep wherein all students read essentially the same material at approximately the same pace irrespective of ability and background—a disadvantage that is considerably overcome in the problems type of course.

As one examines the several types of courses devised by college faculties to meet the needs of general education, it becomes clear that each has considerable merit. The kind of offering adopted will depend on the field involved and the purposes defined by the faculty. The selective type of survey seems especially useful in the sciences, whereas the other types have had greater vogue in the social sciences and humanities. Courses related to problems of personal adjustment, such as preparation for marriage or the psychology of human relations, are usually organized around the problems or the great issues plan.

But whatever the field or the approach devised, general education courses have much in common. They all represent a break from the traditional organization and presentation of subject matter, developing material along lines deemed particularly useful to the student rather than faithful to the discipline. All are concerned with problems of value and ultimate purpose. They insist that the student recognize the importance of values in the formation of judgment and ponder those most appropriate for his own life after reflection on the provocative materials read. Each of the approaches offers courses that stand alone in the sense that they require neither a college prerequisite nor are they in turn a prerequisite to departmental courses following after. Rather they present a segment of human experience for the student's edification and seek to establish a basis for his independent reading thereafter.

All of the courses place emphasis upon good teaching. Since the approach is unorthodox and the students are by definition not professionally interested in the field, the teacher has unusual opportunity for organizing the material in distinctive and interesting fashion. It is a common testimony in colleges where a general education program (of whatever kind) has been worked out, that the entire intellectual life of the campus takes on a new tone and the work in upper level courses is enriched.

In formulating a program of general education, faculties have frequently debated whether a common philosophy should pervade the entire program or whether the different courses can be built on divergent premises. In favor of commonality it is pointed out that there can be greater coherence and interaction throughout the program and the student will more quickly recognize the demands upon him and adapt his efforts to the program objectives. There can be little question but that the curricula at St. John's College, Sarah Lawrence College, Wisconsin's program of Integrated Liberal Studies, and elsewhere which rest upon a single institutional philosophy have achieved a unique character that has brought distinction.

In practice, however, most institutions have adopted a more eclectic plan, permitting the faculty within a given field to work out the course it deems best in light of the peculiarities of that field and the special resources of the staff. Thus, one may find a natural science course operating as a selective survey, a social science course arranged on a problems principle, and a humanities course built around great books or great issues. The advantage here is that each course staff is able to follow its best judgment without being forced into a pattern that it may deem artificial and repugnant. Since it is essential that the teaching faculty should be enthusiastic about the program and constantly working to improve it, this matter of staff autonomy becomes very important. One may conclude that commonality of philosophy is desirable if it can be arrived at agreeably through extensive study and discussion, but that it is not worth the price of low staff morale. Flexibility at this point, with the expectation that staffs will interchange ideas and informally influence one another, is more important than neat consistencies.

FITTING GENERAL EDUCATION INTO THE CURRICULUM

After a faculty has determined the character of its general education courses, it still has the problem of deciding how these courses will relate to the many other offerings of the institution. These curricular questions are essentially the same, irrespective of the type of courses devised, and should be examined in some detail. Only as they are resolved satisfactorily can the program hope to prosper.

Should general education courses be elective or required? From the very beginning of the movement there has been strong sentiment for requiring them. Thus Columbia University required its Contemporary Civilization course forty years ago, and as other courses were developed, these too became mandatory. The college at the University of Chicago developed a standard curriculum of about seventeen courses to be taken by all students virtually without exception. Similarly, at St. John's, the University of Louisville, the Wisconsin program of Integrated Liberal Studies, and other institutions, the student must take all, or practically all, of the courses in their entirety.

It is argued by these institutions that since general education is designed to prepare men for requirements of cultivated and democratic living, and since these requirements are the same for all people irrespective of profession, all should therefore take the program. To permit exceptions would mean to graduate some students with serious gaps in their preparation, and this would be wrong. Moreover, it has been stressed by Robert Hutchins and others that the intellectual world is splitting asunder because men of varying specialties cannot communicate with one another.

Therefore there must be a common base of fundamental training in order that such communication, and hence the solidarity of society, can be preserved. As a practical matter, it is noted also that if all students have a common background, the faculty can depend upon such knowledge in devising advanced courses, whereas if students come from differing backgrounds, the advanced classes will be less efficient and productive.

On the other hand, many faculties have shied away from required general education courses and with reasons that require attention. In the first place it is pointed out that students come from high school with widely varying backgrounds and a course which is a solid fresh experience for one student may be largely repetitious of previous work for others. This is particularly true in recent years as the better high schools have developed strong courses at the junior-senior level, often patterned after those in college. Under such circumstances, it is contended that the college program should be flexible, adapted to the individual backgrounds and abilities of the students, with individual election resting on counseling rather than general prescription for all.

It is also argued that students naturally rebel against required courses and that the morale of a program will inevitably suffer if all students are forced into it. And not only is there a student morale problem, there may be a faculty one as well. If courses are required of all freshmen and sophomores, the numbers involved may be so huge that a choice must be made between very large lecture sections or a multiplicity of normal sized ones. In the first case, there is difficulty in achieving enough student response and interaction to realize the education purposes of the course; and in the second case, so many faculty are required that it is difficult to get competent and dedicated persons for the task.

The politics of the campus may also help determine this matter of prescription. When the several departments believe strongly that their elementary courses are as good for general education purposes as the newly devised ones, it may be difficult to get majority approval of a required program, whereas faculty members may accept an optional arrangement permitting the student to choose. Similarly, in a university where there are a number of technical colleges, those faculties may be unwilling to divert student time for the full general education program whereas they will endorse a limited number of courses.

With such persuasive arguments on both sides of the prescriptive issue, it is inevitable that many faculties should seek a compromise. One device has been to offer a series of courses, say seven, and then permit the student to choose five or six from that number. Thus there would be a substantial amount of common background among the students and yet a measure of free election. Such a plan was employed at Michigan State University although in 1954 that institution changed to a core of required courses. A variant on this arrangement is to require a year's course in a broad field such as the humanities or the social sciences and then to offer several integrated courses in each field which can be elected to satisfy the requirement. This plan is in effect, for example, at Harvard.

Another compromise arrangement involves extensive use of achievement examinations. A program of courses is required but the student is encouraged to study independently and prepare himself to pass an examination over the material. This device is particularly suitable where high schools are developing courses of virtually college quality. If the student achieves a passing score on the examination he is exempted from the requirement and with a very high score may even be given college credit for the course.

The issue of prescription versus election has not yet been resolved. In general, prescription tends to prevail for those programs based on a neo-humanist or rationalist philosophy whereas election is more common for programs of an instrumentalist nature. The latter are more student-centered and hence are more ready to adapt to individual differences. If one can discern a trend, it is toward a continuation of requirements, with perhaps some internal election such as at Harvard, and increased utilization of achievement tests to speed the superior student on into advanced work.

Should the program be organized on a two-year or a four-year basis? There has been a tendency in many institutions to organize a program for freshmen and sophomores, assuming that they can then go on to specialized work in the several departments and professional schools. The courses thus serve as a foundation to give a broad orientation and help the student to choose his profession wisely and see it in perspective. It is pointed out also that about half the college students do not proceed beyond the sophomore year. If they begin a specialized program early and then abandon it, they suffer a serious waste of time, whereas a general education program is relevant to the student's needs irrespective of his subsequent employment. A common experience during the first two years will likewise help to establish an intellectual community which will unite the students throughout college years even though their specialized paths may diverge.

On the other hand, many faculties insist that both the general and the vocational programs should continue for the full college period. They point out that the student usually comes with a strong vocational drive and it is psychologically unwise to deny him work in his chosen field until he has reached the junior year. Rather, he should be able to take at least one course with vocational purpose during his freshman year and all work will then profit from his improved morale and motivation. Moreover, he needs early try-out experiences to determine whether his proposed vocational goal is sound or should be shifted, and for some professions such as medicine he almost certainly must begin his departmental science work during the freshman year. Similarly, it is contended that the general education experience should be spread through four years, for some of the courses require a kind of abstraction and maturity not found in the typical underclassman. Indeed, some universities continue these courses on into the graduate school.

Frequently at the senior or graduate levels, the general education course takes a different turn. Instead of being introductory to a field it serves as a capstone to help the student tie together the many aspects of his four year college experience. There are many integrating themes around which a climactic course of this kind can be built; for example, the impact of science upon civilization, problems of social control in modern society, or (as at Antioch) the autobiography of the student's own intellectual development. Sometimes these synthesizing courses are designed primarily for majors and seek to integrate the work of a single department, while in other cases they have a more general education flavor enabling the student to gain a new grasp of the complex web of life.

On this matter of timing, a resolution seems in sight. More and more colleges are adopting a compromise arrangement whereby students have a preponderance of general education during the first year with perhaps one course related to the anticipated vocation. Then during the four years the general education component will continue in diminishing amount while increasing time is given to specialized work and free electives. This arrangement graphically symbolizes the point that general education is not an abrupt experience designed for 18 and 19 year olds. Rather it is a part of life's total growth beginning in infancy and continuing to the grave, simply having a special crescendo and systematization during the early years in college.

Should general education courses be inter-related? It is often suggested that if the purpose of general education is to give the student a rounded view of life, then the several courses should themselves be interwoven in such fashion that they tell a connected and coherent story. Thus Alexander Meiklejohn's Experimental College which flourished at the University of Wisconsin from 1927 to 1932 integrated all freshman work around various facets of Greek civilization—humanistic, social, and scientific. The following year, the students studied another historical period in its manifold relationships. A somewhat similar device has been developed at the Boston University General College with faculty members from the several courses working zealously to develop connections with the others. There the staff is organized into teams with a natural scientist, a social scientist, and a humanist sharing the same office and dealing with the same students in their respective sections, thus insuring that there will be a cooperative and interconnected approach to the year's work.

While the idea has considerable appeal, it does not seem to have caught on widely. There are many difficulties. Faculties have found that the integration of material within a single course has so taxed their time and ingenuity that there has been no ambition left for super-integrations. Moreover, the chronological device which has usually been the major coordinating principle is not equally appropriate for all fields. It works well in the humanities but is usually rejected by the natural scientist and social scientist who wish to devote most time to the contemporary facts and issues of their field. They regard a forced marriage with the humanities as an artificial and misdirected effort.

While the close coordination of all general education courses has not gained wide favor, there is a growing tendency for general education staffs to communicate with one another and to discover those topical interconnections that can be demonstrated naturally. The establishment of these correlations wherever possible helps the student to relate his knowledge and gain mutual reinforcement from the several courses. As existing courses become more firmly established, the staffs can find time to explore interrelationships and one may expect considerable progress in this direction.

How can general education be articulated with previous high school training and with subsequent college courses? The problem of articulation is one of the most pressing in higher education today. Almost every curriculum analyst agrees that there is considerable duplication of work between high school and college in some fields and serious gaps in others. In American history, for example, the college course may begin with 1492 and follow the development of America chronologically to the present time, introducing some new material but actually offering few new insights not emphasized by a good high school teacher (perhaps trained under this same college instructor!). Allowance is usually made for previous high school work in such subjects as higher algebra and foreign language, but for the most part college courses proceed on the assumption that the student has had little or no previous learning in the subject. For the weak student this assumption is pragmatically valid but for the good student first-year college work may be repetitious and boring. Testing students and exempting the best ones from elementary general education courses is a partial solution, as suggested above, but it does not fully solve the problem. Even the best student has imperfect command of American history, or any other field, and the problem is therefore partially curricular—to devise courses that the most able students will find both challenging and rewarding.

A solution to this problem lies in extensive discussion among elementary, secondary, and college teachers to determine the proper responsibility of education at each stage. If in the fields of English expression, history and the social sciences, the natural sciences, and other subjects, teachers could agree upon a continuum of development most appropriate for their field, their work in each stage could be better articulated with that below. Indeed, recognizing that some students will inevitably progress faster than others, it may be possible to differentiate assignments and projects to enable varying students in the same class to proceed from a common minimal core of subject matter to as much enrichment as each can achieve. But all this implies an analysis of materials and learning theory, together with a spirit of cooperation among the many levels, that is now only beginning to emerge in educational planning. Much more needs to be done.

Somewhat the same problem arises between basic college courses in general education and advanced departmental courses. When the student takes a freshman integrated course in the social sciences (learning, incidentally, considerable economics and sociology and government), if he is thereby inspired to advanced work, must he then take the beginning principles course in the department selected—with some inevitable duplication? Or can he go on at once to upper level courses? The same problem arises in the natural sciences and to some extent in the humanities. Usually the answer has been that the student is not prepared for advanced courses and must take the introductory departmental offering. The matter is of course simplified in those elective systems where students are encouraged not to take the integrated general education course in the field of their proposed major but rather to proceed at once to the introductory departmental offering. In institutions where general education courses are prescribed, there have been efforts, some of them quite successful, for redesigning subsequent departmental courses on a somewhat higher level than normal. This arrangement takes account of the common general education background and avoids serious duplication. In this instance, as in articulation with high schools, the responsibility for adjustment lies primarily at the upper level, for any lower-level attempt at adjustment to succeeding courses will almost surely vitiate their general education purpose.

The articulation problem raises another issue which has been too long neglected in educational planning. This is the relation between detail and generalization. Critics of general education will sometimes argue that it is wrong to have broad integrated courses at the lower college levels before the student has had a solid foundation in the subject matter of various fields. They contend that highly discrete and fact-laden courses should be taught in the early years with the integrated courses left to the senior or graduate level when the student has acquired solid knowledge upon which to build his generalizations. The argument has some appeal and it will be remembered that general educationists themselves have been among the first to pioneer supplementary integrated courses at advanced levels. But the theory really has little basis in practical experience. It is unrealistic to expect that American youth will continue to memorize huge quantities of information before searching out their meaning, and if it were attempted, the residue of remembered material would be quite insufficient for sound generalization when the "pay-off day" arrived.

In truth, education is a constant interaction between factual acquisition and generalization from the time of infancy on. The little child develops the generalized concept of "tree" before he distinguishes details of the oak tree, birch, or maple. He recognizes a house before he can identify a bungalow, ranch-type, or

Cape Cod. But as he gains new information, his previous generalizations are constantly refined and made more valid. As Whitehead points out in *The Aims of Education,* education is a spiraling process whereby one moves steadily from fact to theory to further fact to expanded theory and so on throughout life. At the college level, the student comes with an enormous background of previously learned fact and developed theory, some sound and useful and some inaccurate and shallow. It is a job of the general education course to accelerate the growing process by providing still further information and encouraging sounder and broader generalizations. And these hopefully may be further developed in the advanced courses that follow.

Now it is obvious that generalizations expounded without substantial factual background become sheer verbalisms, which the student may memorize for examination purposes but which he will never understand well enough to use in practical experience. On the other hand, if he is forced to go far in memorizing material without perceiving the point, he will soon lose interest. The challenge to the general education teacher, as to all others, is to assess accurately the varying backgrounds of informational mastery and theoretical sophistication with which students come and to push them forward along the next stage of the spiral. And there are little spirals within the larger ones. On any new topic there is a progression from the what to the how to the why—from description to analysis to theoretical insight—similar to the progression of one's total intellectual development. The general education course that jumps to generalization without adequate factual background or that dwells too long on facts without proceeding to generalized meaning is certain to fail. Herein lies a constant pedagogical challenge.

INTELLECTUAL PROBLEMS OF GENERAL EDUCATION

One cannot conclude a discussion of general education programs without recognizing some of the intellectual issues that still challenge the movement. These center primarily around the problems of integration, and two in particular must be examined.

Is interdisciplinary integration essential to general education? This question has sharply divided faculties in the past. The integrationists argue that since a major function of general education is to give the student perspective over a broad field in the one or two courses available to him, all related disciplines must be brought together in the courses or such perspective will be denied. It is argued also that in the very process of integration common principles and relationships among the disciplines will be identified and the learning made more efficient.

On the other hand, stalwarts in traditional departments contend that the chief purpose of general education is not to give intellectual perspective but rather to help the student understand the processes of human living and this can be as well done by a good course in history or philosophy or sociology or literature as it can in one of the interdisciplinary courses.

The issue here seems to be a conflict between the good and the better, always a difficult matter to resolve and particularly when vested interests may be involved. The general education value of many departmental courses must surely be conceded, assuming equality of instructional competence. And for students who enter college with a good testable grasp of materials in the integrated course, immediate referral to one of the departmental offerings is to be recommended. Such students, however, are probably a small minority and for the rest a good integrated course will give the student both the perspective and the intellectual challenge that he needs.

The question re-raises the semantic need to distinguish between general and liberal education. If general education is regarded as a pursuit of those elemental ideas required for mature responsible living while liberal education includes those additional studies which are desirable but not essential for everyone, the issue may be partially resolved. By this definition, general education is simply a phase of liberal education, a seasoning in the fundamentals, while liberal education moves a student further along such paths as his personal interests may direct. All these elements are important in the student's development, though for general education purposes the core of integrated courses—if soundly conceived and imaginatively taught—would seem to be preferable. Incidentally, some of the traditional departments have developed courses that are virtually interdisciplinary in nature—such as history which may depict Man's intellectual and social as well as political development, or human anthropology which looks at the totality of his culture. If designed for the general student, such courses should surely be included among the integrated offerings of general education. However, their integration is limited in scope and hence subject to many of the objections noted for distribution requirements earlier in this chapter.

Does general education have a responsibility for creative scholarship? The general education movement is occasionally deplored on the ground that it affords little intellectual challenge to either students or staff but rather is a rehash of truths already propounded by pioneers in the component disciplines. It is argued that strong minds will avoid assignment to general education teaching because they prefer to work out on the frontier of some discipline where there is excitement in discovering new truths.

Fortunately there is another side to the matter. While it is true that empirical research tends to move forward on a tiny segment of the specialty, such research is not confined to specialists. Many general education professors maintain their particular research interests alongside their general education teaching. But their unique contribution to scholarship lies in their ability, and indeed necessity, for synthesis. With particles of new knowledge appearing constantly in all the disciplines, it is essential that some persons devote themselves to the task of interpreting these research findings and showing their relationships. The discovery of a new gestalt wherein factual data are reorganized around new concepts and meanings is a critically important function in modern scholarship. Not only does it provide the only hope for maintaining some overall coherence within the intellectual world, but it also is an indispensable means for interpreting findings to the lay public.

Professors of general education, because of their constant reading in several disciplines, develop the kind of searching minds required for formulating new concepts. In the process they not only derive new insights for their courses but serve as coordinators and catalysts for the specialized researchers as well.

Such general education scholars serve much the same function as the diagnostician in modern medicine who works with many specialists and arrives at conclusions that no specialist could have reached alone. The situation reminds one of the three fabled blind men, each of whom studied one part of the elephant; they discovered a rope, a tree, and a wall but were unable to perceive that the animal was an organic whole, a living entity with unique character and purpose. That required a synthesist.

The general education professor may make use of such divergent elements as Freudian psychology, cultural anthropology, and political dynamics to illuminate the study of a fascist state. Or he may examine the growth of a child in terms of its biological development, its social adjustment, its religious nature, and its intellectual maturity. The basic problems of life do not fit neatly into the artificially organized disciplines of the scholars but rather involve them all. And often the key to the problem may lie among the interstitial spaces outside any of the established scholarly compartments.

The general education professor therefore has a distinct and inescapable responsibility in the world of modern scholarship. While he must be first of all a good teacher, there is a constant obligation to read widely and venture fresh, even daring, conceptions. It is clear that general education is no place for limited or timid minds. The job of discovering and preparing faculty members for work in general education goes beyond the scope of the present chapter but is crucial to the continued development and vitality of the movement.

Chapter IV

TEACHING IN GENERAL EDUCATION

SIDNEY J. FRENCH
Dean of the College of Basic Studies
University of South Florida

A MEDICAL doctor studies not only medicine but the art of the practice as well. He spends a year or more interning before he is regarded as worthy and qualified to hang out his shingle.

A lawyer studies not only the law but the art of his practice as well. He must learn how to argue, to question and cross-question in order to bring out the proper evidence, and to summarize in a way which will do the most for his client.

Indeed, all learned professions except one include some study of the art of the practice as well as the subject matter of the profession. That one is college teaching! Here it seems to be assumed that the person who knows the subject matter of his field possesses, intuitively, the art of teaching it.

Historically, the reason for this anomaly is simple. The typical requirement for college teaching has been and is the degree of Doctor of Philosophy. This degree, developed in Europe, principally in Germany, is a research degree. Those achieving it were expected to carry on research in their field. But, since research was carried on largely within the walls of the universities, the professional researcher was expected to train other researchers in his field as well. Somewhat incidentally, he was a teacher. The university paid his salary for the teaching he did and allowed him time to carry on his research. In addition he had advanced students to assist him with further research. It was an ideal arrangement for the professor.

This German system was transposed to America in the latter part of the nineteenth century with the starting of the first American graduate school at The Johns Hopkins University. Thus, a system appropriate for German universities was superimposed upon an educational system very different from it.

Whereas German universities are essentially graduate schools, there are no institutions in Germany comparable to the American liberal arts undergraduate colleges. This level of education in Germany is supplied by the Gymnasium.

Essentially, then, we adopted the form without the substance. We adopted but failed to adapt. We insisted on the Ph. D. degree for our college teachers, but their principal job was not research, it was to teach at the undergraduate level. While somewhat oversimplified this is, in essence, what has happened.

The situation has been further complicated by the spectacular rise of American normal schools and teachers' colleges in the latter part of the nineteenth century. These, as public institutions, exerted strong influence on the pattern for preparation for elementary and secondary school teachers. They were accused of substituting methods for substance. The reaction to this at the college level was distinctly negative; it was to avoid anything which smacked of Education with a capital "E." The college teacher, it was argued, was a pure subject matter specialist and should not be contaminated by taking education courses.

We confused college education in America with university education in Europe—from whence have come so many of our customs and traditions—and yet the two are far from comparable.

The American liberal arts college is unique. Stemming from Europe, to be sure, it partook more of the liberal character of Oxford and Cambridge than of the professional universities of Germany and continental Europe. Starting early in American civilization, it has developed its own character and has no real counterpart in any other part of the world. It is largely the product of the American Christian churches. All over the country were established these small church-related colleges, principally, in early days, to train an educated ministry. Many of them are now among the great institutions of learning in America. They preceded the state universities by many years and have continuously influenced the pattern of American higher education. Today, nearly half of American college youth attend these private institutions. The state universities, while usually more diversified, offer essentially the same pattern of liberal education as do the private institutions.

Unlike professional education in many respects, liberal education deals with areas and problems of our culture, technology, and heritage, while general education deals with those aspects and skills which should be held in common by all educated people. The professionally educated as well as the liberally educated person should know and understand our heritage and the problems common to civilization today.

For some years there has been a definite trend in liberal arts colleges toward the inclusion of more professional work while the professional schools are broadening their programs to include more liberal and general education. We find that many teachers trained as subject-matter specialists are now expected to teach students at the undergraduate level whose interest is in general and liberal more than in professional education. It is not enough to be able to hand out subject matter in a learned way. Indeed, this is *not* the principal function of the college teacher. To be sure, he must know his subject matter, but he must be able, as well, to deal with it in ways which indicate its relationships to other areas and to our cultural heritage.

In training for a profession, motivation can usually be assumed and even poor teaching may not destroy such motivation. In liberal education, on the other hand, strong motivation does not normally exist. It must be developed. Hence, the *art* of teaching assumes real importance. The teacher trained in subject-matter and research will need to augment such training by an understanding of the psychology of motivation, by experimentation with new ways to present material, to involve students, to make the subject interesting even though it may be technical, and to do all of this without the charge that he is making it superficial. This calls for teaching skill. And unfortunately, because of our failure to prepare college teachers to teach, this must be developed on the job at the expense of the students. Many young Ph. D.'s are naively unaware that such things are a part of college teaching.

What has been said about the art of teaching in liberal education applies with greater significance to the field of general education. One may think of good college education today as involving a continuum starting with general education and moving through liberal to professional studies. Striking the proper balance is one of the tasks American higher education faces. There has been much complaint, for example, that engineering education is too narrow and the engineer is a "one track" product. The same charge has been made about medical education, teacher education, business education, agriculture, and most of the other professional programs. Definite efforts are being made to introduce larger amounts of general and liberal education to these programs.

On the other hand, in an effort to get away from too highly professionalized programs there has been a tendency in some quarters to place great emphasis on general and liberal education almost to the exclusion of professional objectives. This is exemplified most clearly today in the program of St. John's College, which claims no professional aims, offers no majors, but devotes itself entirely to a program taken in common by all students and using the "great books" approach.

Just as there is a continuum from general to professional studies, so too we need a continuum of teachers prepared to teach in various parts of the program. In a sense the type of skills needed varies in inverse proportion to the progression of the continuum. That is to say, the teacher teaching general education will need to know and practice the *arts of teaching* more than the teacher teaching, say surgery of the mouth, or electronic systems. The latter are teaching advanced students highly motivated in terms of the subject matter and deeply concerned with mastery of the technique involved. The teacher must know his subject and be skilled in the techniques of the practice and their demonstration. The kind of skill needed differs from that required in teaching, for example, an integrated course in the physical or social sciences, even though both involve mastery of the subject matter concerned.

There are a number of recognized techniques for effective teaching at the college level. While these apply generally to the entire continuum, they apply most specifically to general education.

It is no doubt true that great teachers are born, not made. They seem to have, instinctively, the necessary teaching skills and know just as instinctively how to use them. They may never have had a course in education or psychology but they have a love of subject, a breadth of interest, and a concern for students as human beings which makes them great teachers.

There are several kinds of greatness in teaching. Some, perhaps the most spectacular teachers, have been great lecturers. Some have been wise counselors, some have been able leaders of discussion, stimulating their students to activity on their own account. Some have been great human beings, beloved by generations of students; others have won great respect for their knowledge and incisiveness, but not love. Some teach subjects; all teach students. As Clifton Fadiman has said of Mark Van Doren, "Mr. Van Doren of course taught English in the sense that he did not teach mathematics; but his real subject was one on which no examination could test you: human life."[1]

There is, of course, a tendency for a young college teacher to imitate some one of his teachers whom he admires greatly. This may extend, at times, to the adoption of his mannerisms. There is nothing wrong with this and much good, but it may well be that this young teacher does not have the same talents and thus fails to do good teaching by such methods. He is, moreover, unaware that there *are other* methods. Since lecturing is by far the most common practice among college teachers, the young teacher will usually feel more comfortable and competent if he too lectures. By so doing he can control the situation. By limiting himself to the areas of his competence he avoids exposing ignorance and avoids questions he might not be able to answer. He can fill up the necessary fifty minutes even though he may merely cover and expand slightly on the material of the textbook. The situation in which he is teaching may call for an entirely different approach. Not realizing this, he goes on lecturing, often destroying any latent interest his students might have.

While it may be true that great teachers are born and teach inspirationally by instinct, it is equally true that teachers not so great (and there are many more of these) can learn to teach more effectively if they are conscious that there are techniques of good teaching and if they are willing to experiment with them.

There are a number of approaches to effective teaching methods but these do not fall into neat categories. They do differ from one another in degree sufficiently to be described here as separate approaches.

For our purposes these are broken down as follows:

The Formal Lecture
The Informal Lecture
The Discussion
The Case Method
The Team Approach
The "Block and Gap" Plan
The Problem Approach
The Student Centered Approach
The Use of Visual Aids

The Formal Lecture. Since this method is so widely used in both large and small institutions, it is considered first. What are the attributes of a good lecture; what are the qualities of a good lecturer? In what kinds of classes should lectures be used; in what kinds should they not be used?

The writer was once a member of a physics class enrolling five students. We sat on stools before a laboratory table. The teacher stood across the table and lectured the full period with a voice which carried literally to all parts of the building. To make matters worse he had a "spraying" voice and often came within "range" when making a point. This was, obviously, not the place for a formal lecture, but the teacher knew no other way.

The lecture has been used as a device to handle large numbers of students economically. In spite of attacks by those who say that it merely conveys information from the teacher's notes to the students' notebooks, there is much to be said for the lecture when properly used. It obviously should not merely repeat the text as is too often the case. The lecturer's notes should be destroyed and rewritten at least once a year. No student generation should be able to pass along its notes to the next class with the idea that they would still be useful. (And most certainly the jokes should be changed.) Some good lecturers work from a minimum outline and some put their outline on the board either before or during the lecture.

The adroit lecturer will leave his students with problems to solve. He will provide certain evidence, raise certain questions, point out certain possible conclusions, and leave the students to pursue the matter further and reach their own conclusions. In general education courses this approach is particularly significant if the course is built around problems. The trouble with many lecturers is that they insist on providing all the answers, leaving nothing for the students to do.

In many courses the lecture is only one part of the course, supplemented by discussion meetings of smaller groups. In general education the lecture in such courses has been effectively used for (1) the introduction of new subjects or problems, and (2) the transition from one field to another.

Another way of using the lecture effectively in a general education course is to reverse the function of the lecture. Instead of supplementing the lecture by discussion meetings, the lecture may be used to bring together and summarize the results of discussion meetings. The lecture supplements rather than being, itself, supplemented. This, of course, is a matter of emphasis and the situation should be flexible enough to use the lecture in several ways in the same course.

The lecturer in a large course should be chosen for his skill in lecturing. He should have a good speaking voice, should regard his assignment as of the utmost importance, should invite the criticism of his colleagues, and should work at trying to improve his effectiveness both in presentation and in skillful, suspenseful organization of material. He should regard this assignment as one in which the prime purpose is to present the material in a way to interest students and command their attention, respect, and curiosity, rather than to "cover the ground." He can be something of a "showman." This is a skill not many college teachers possess. Too often it is taken for granted that the senior professor will do the lecturing, even though he may be a mumbler and a bumbler. He might have great skill in leading a discussion or in directing research, but for the sake of academic prestige he must also be the lecturer. We need better ways of using the skills we are blessed with or can develop. It is no disgrace not to be a great lecturer; it is a disgrace to try to lecture if one is a poor lecturer.

No statistical study has ever been, or probably could be, made of the number of student hours "lost" in American higher education due to poor lecturing, but the number must run into the millions annually. College students have learned to accept the inevitable. They have learned to shut off their minds—or worse yet, to take copious notes on material they could read in the textbook.

Of equal importance with good lecturing is the preparation of students to know what to look for and record from a good lecture. Indiscriminate note taking in lectures is both a curse on our system and a waste of valuable student time. There are great differences of receptivity to lectures. Some students learn well through lectures. Sometimes this is due to the challenge presented; sometimes (and more often) it is the easiest way to learn and saves reading the textbook. Many students boast they do not need to "crack the book." This is prima faci evidence of the failure of the lecture to do what it should do. Other students get little or nothing from lectures. They should be taught what to look for and how to take good notes. A simple device for doing this by example is to have an instructor take notes on the blackboard while listening to another instructor lecture. One or two examples of this sort will establish a good pattern of note taking for most students.

Some large institutions have proposed giving students in general education courses the choice of taking the course in a series of lectures or taking it in smaller discussion groups with permission to shift from one to the other type in order to discover which is most effective for them. Indeed, recent evidence suggests that many students do about as well when turned loose with their books and supplementary materials.

Suffice it to say that the formal lecture is somewhat limited in the things it can accomplish. It should be used with discretion and used only by those who have or can develop skill in lecturing. Its object should not be to cover the facts and materials normally found in the textbook but rather to open up avenues, present challenges, propose hypotheses, and in general stimulate students to go forward on their own more deeply into the problems presented.

The Informal Lecture. No method of teaching at the college level is more commonly used than the informal lecture. It has many features to recommend it. It can be successful in general, liberal, and professional studies alike. While there seems to be no optimum class size in which this method operates best, it is usually used in classes of less than one hundred and often with very small classes.

In superficial ways the informal lecture class resembles the discussion class; students are free to talk. However, it is usually more highly structured. The informality lies in the fact that students may interrupt the lecturer from time to time. Of course, it is often a favorite pastime of some students to try to divert the lecturer so that he will stray afield and not cover the allotted span of pages. Thus, the new assignment must be reduced in length.

Usually the lecturer is interrupted only when a student fails to understand something said rather than to raise significant questions. In fact, the real weakness of the method is that the student is seldom prepared to raise significant questions; he is too busy following the lecturer and taking notes. The lecture is usually informational in nature covering the material in the textbook or enlarging on it. It is less well prepared than the formal lecture and often "rambles." Students can more easily avoid "cracking the book" under this system than under the formal lecture plan.

Many teachers, discovering that students are not prepared, turn more and more to lecturing. The student, realizing that he can thus get the material without reading the book, ceases to prepare, and a vicious circle is created, forcing the teacher to do more and more lecturing. A short quiz at the beginning of the hour will often avoid this.

In general education, the informal lecture as usually misused is hardly adequate. We are less concerned with coverage than we are in dealing with a few typical problems. Students should become involved in these problems and in the search for their own solutions. The approach should be less informational than quizzical. It is, of course, true that we must not ignore significant information pertinent to the problem, and there will be occasions when the informational lecture, either formal or informal, is clearly indicated. The skillful teacher is the one who knows when to pick up this ball and run with it. Especially, there is a time for the ten-minute "lecturette," to use a term coined at the Harvard Graduate School of Business Administration, but the instructor must not forget to toss the ball back before crossing the goal line. It is the students who should make the touchdowns. This is their game.

The Discussion Method. Theoretically, at least, the discussion method reverses the process of the informal lecture. The teacher may interrupt the students from time to time. There is, perhaps, no term more abused and less understood than the "discussion method." Use and misuse of this method varies all the way from the non-structured discussion involving group dynamics to the old fashioned recitation or quiz. In many instances instructors claiming to use the discussion method are actually lecturing with an occasional question thrown to students. Teachers willing to use a tape recorder in class have often discovered to their chagrin that they have been doing nine-tenths of the talking. The discussion has been a monologue.

One great weakness of the discussion method is failure on the part of students to prepare for the discussion. Another is the inability of the teacher to lead a good discussion. There is little to be gained from a group of unprepared students sitting around a table with an unimaginative teacher. This usually forces the instructor to do the talking; the discussion becomes a virtual lecture and we are in the vicious circle. Students can, indeed, through a sort of sit-tight strike, easily destroy the effectiveness of a discussion class. The teacher can destroy it even more effectively if he knows nothing about leading a good discussion.

Nevertheless, a well led discussion class can be highly stimulating and in certain areas of general education the technique is almost imperative. Leading a discussion group requires a great deal of skill—and restraint. The college teacher is too apt to want to tell the answers since he usually knows them. It is painful for him to sit with students and watch them grope for understanding. The leader has constantly to tell himself that speed is not important and that the only way for a student to reach meaningful understanding is to find it for himself. The thrill and permanence of self-discovery justify any lack of speed. The leader needs to understand and practice the art of reflecting ideas around the table, of mirroring comments directly, of leading without seeming to direct, providing clues without providing answers, providing encouragement of expression without promoting garrulity, and demanding clarity without provoking silence. He must know when to include a "lecturette," when to lead the discussion back to the main line, and when to let it take its head.

To lead a good discussion class requires the greatest skill in college teaching. Yet most new college instructors come to their jobs with no comprehension whatever that such skill is important in college teaching, and no idea how to attain it.

While it is not always true that a great lecturer is a poor discussion leader, it is often the case. Teachers who enjoy lecturing often find it difficult to keep from talking. Good discussion leaders, for the opposite reason, may be poor lecturers. We should make it possible for teachers to do what they can do best in order to make the greatest contribution to the profession. Good discussion leaders are as rare as good lecturers. Each should be used in his own sphere.

The Case Method. The case method is a specific application of the discussion method to a unique situation. It is used in a number of different ways. To understand its effectiveness one must understand the meaning of the term "case" as used here. The "case" is the history of an actual occurrence so disguised that the actual participants, organizations, and locale are not revealed. A "case" may be prepared by skilled interviewer-case writers who talk to those concerned and put together the events, including some of the conversations, opinions, and actions of the principal participants. Usually the case concerns a problem in human relations which may involve industrial, political, ethical, economic, and sociological facets. It deals with the problems and events but includes no "solution." In this respect it differs from cases used in many law schools. The case may vary in length from two or three mimeographed pages to several hundred. As defined here, the cases are "small" specific case histories rather than large more generalized cases such as "The Problem of Political Stability in France" or the "Supreme Court and Desegregation."

The case method as here defined has evolved largely from the use of cases in the Harvard Graduate School of Business Administration developed under the leadership of the late Dean Wallace B. Donham. Extended first to use in human relations courses, the method has also been used in courses in history, the social sciences, and psychology. The "purest" use is to be found in human relations courses, since this field is not complicated by the terminology of a discipline.

The objectives of a course built around such cases usually are to lead students to a better understanding of how such problems arise, how they are dealt with by different individuals who see them from differing points of view, how emotional response may color the facts and affect the solutions, and how decisions may be reached by group discussion. Such a course provides the mental therapy for the students if nothing more. At its best it provides the student with a deeper understanding of human problems, with the ability to distinguish emotional response from reason, fact from fabrication, and clear thinking from fuzzy. In short, it provides, through dealing with a number of such situations, a better way of thinking about social problems.

The success of the case method depends heavily upon the skill and interest of the teacher. He must have all of the attributes of the skilled discussion leader, and in addition must understand and practice non-directive techniques. Here, if ever, the teacher must keep his mouth shut. He must understand clearly the objectives he is seeking for the students. The success of the method depends equally on the willingness of students to participate in such a venture and their preparation for discussing a case. At first the students unused to this method tend to regard such a course as a mere "bull-session." Soon the more perceptive begin to sense the objectives and the values to be attained; the others gradually follow. If the success of a course can be measured by the amount of discussion provoked outside the classroom, this method can be successful because many of the cases become continuing subjects of heated campus and dormitory discussion.

Use of the case method in general education has been made at a number of institutions. At Colgate University the freshman social science course was taught entirely by this method for several years. Experimentation and the results there suggest, however, that a course taught by this method at the freshman level needs some "leavening" with more orthodox materials. Some students complained, for example, that they didn't "learn anything"; that they didn't know what to study for the final examination; that they had nothing to write down in their notebooks; that they "got" nothing from the instructor who instead of "teaching" them merely remained silent. The use of the "lecturette," the grouping of cases to lead up to a more generalized problem, and the consideration, finally, of some of these broader problems can provide some of the "leaven" needed.

There are a number of other ways in which such cases can be used in general education. They can be used, for instance, to introduce a new phase of the course, or as a specific application at the end of a more general topic. But unless they are used with some consistency younger students, at least, do not sense the significance of the method or the possible outcomes. The use of this method in general education has great promise, and further experimentation with it is clearly indicated.

A different concept of the case approach has been used successfully at Harvard in science. The course was originally developed under the leadership of President James B. Conant. The cases used are "large" cases, each involving the historical development of some one of the major concepts of science. A number of such cases have been published. The student follows the chronological development of the concept through the experiments and conclusions of the principal contributors. For example, in the development of the modern concept of combustion the student first studies the older theory of phlogiston sufficiently to understand it. He then studies the work of Lavoisier and Priestley bearing on the problem. He notes the judgments made, the errors, the near-misses, the groping, the interpretations of the results, and the way in which the work of one man may impinge upon or contribute to that of another. Thus, he learns how scientists attempt to solve their problems. The use of historical cases involves simple techniques and instruments which the general student can understand. A weakness of the method for general education purposes, however, is that it does deal entirely in historical cases while most students want to know something about atomic energy, synthetic products, and other modern scientific developments.

Nevertheless, such cases have many things to commend their use in general education. They can be used in conjunction with the study of principles, as application, as illustrations of types of problems met with, as ends in themselves, and as illustration of the ways in which the several disciplines are interdependent when applied to the problems of men.

The Team Approach. Little has yet been written about the team method of teaching general education. In principle it is an ideal approach; in practice it presents a number of difficulties.

In the more successful general education courses a class is taught through a whole semester or year by one instructor. The alternative is to use a succession of instructors, each dealing with his own specialty. In this instance the course is broken into "specialized" blocks following one another. This approach has not, in general, proved successful since each block is studied in isolation of its relationship to the other blocks and there is no real integration. It is also an anomalous situation in which teachers who are specialists teach students who are supposed to be generalists.

The more successful plan is that in which each instructor teaches his section through the semester or year even though he may not be a specialist in some of the areas or blocks he is teaching. A team of instructors made up of "specialists" from the several areas dealt with in the course meets frequently for staff sessions in which each specialist in turn "instructs" the others in the problems involving his field. Such a team using the case method, for example, will often have a full discussion of the case to be used in advance of the class session. Incidentally, this method provides a fine broadening education for the faculty involved and often creates both respect for and interest in the other man's field. It has been said, only half in jest, that the faculty members get more education than the students. This type of team approach might be termed the "horizontal" approach.

The term "team approach," however, usually refers to a newer development, using a "vertical" approach. Here the team is composed of at least one member from each of the several courses included in the general education program. Ideally, all members of the team are teaching the same set of students. For example, if there are five general education courses required of all students, there will be five faculty members on a team. Students will be assigned to sections in each course such that the same students will have all five members of a particular team as their teachers.

The five team members share an office, or offices, and one serves as chairman or leader of the team. They meet frequently, maintaining close coordination between the several courses, eliminating unnecessary overlap, establishing appropriate emphases, informing one another of successful devices and techniques of teaching, and, in general, educating one another.

Obviously, one of the most important assets of this approach lies in the possibilities of student guidance. Indeed, as it is used in the Junior College of Boston University this is an important function of the team approach. Since the five members of the team teach the same students they come to know them all well. Students are discussed frequently. They are free to go to any member of the team for advice and counsel. Students having academic difficulties are "caught" early. Those with mental or emotional problems are likewise identified early and can be referred to competent advisers. In particular, the team approach as used at Boston University makes possible the early selection and guidance of students capable of going on into upper-division work.

Aside from its counseling value where arrangements can be such that all members of a team are teaching the same students, there is much to be said for the "vertical" team for other reasons. While we tend to get fairly good coordination within a given general education course, the sections of which are taught by a "horizontal" team, there is often very little knowledge by the staff of one course about what is being done in another course in the same program. Indeed, this can be charged as a common weakness of most general education programs. Vertical team seminars meeting regularly, to exchange ideas and find out what is going on in each of the several courses, could do much to overcome this weakness, and at the same time provide team members with a better understanding of the whole program, its weaknesses, strengths, and objectives. This coordination at the work level is far more important than technical coordination at the "summit."

With both horizontal and vertical coordination through teams the possibilities of real integration loom large.

There are other ways of using a team approach. In one program recently proposed, for example, two comprehensive courses, one in science and mathematics, and one in the social sciences and humanities (including language), constituted the whole of the freshman year. Ideally, the whole freshman year would be taught by the team method, one team handling the science-mathematics, the other handling the social science-humanities. This scheme combines, in part, the horizontal and vertical approaches.

The Block and Gap Plan. Professor Eric Rogers of Princeton has brought the term "block and gap" into usage in general education courses. It is a self-descriptive term which can be applied to other courses as well. Rather than attempt to "cover" a field he advocates the rather intensive study of certain blocks within a field and the frank omission of others which may be equally important but which, in the time allotted, could not be covered adequately. Another term applied to this type of course is "deep-sampling."

The earlier charges against the survey courses in general education were based on the fact that they attempted to cover too much ground and were therefore superficial. The "block and gap" plan not only eliminates this weakness but gives the student a better and deeper conception of some typical problems of the field. The term may be applied to single-discipline courses such as the physics course in general education given by Professor Rogers,[2] or to multi-discipline courses in which the blocks selected may cross the lines of several disciplines.

The Problem Approach. Very similar to the "block and gap" plan is the problem approach. It differs, however, in dealing with problems rather than blocks. A problem is posed. The evidence is gathered and examined. Solutions are proposed. This method has the advantage, when well used, of getting the students themselves deeply involved in the solution of real problems.

In a sense this approach is similar to the case method where the cases used are "large" rather than small. It differs from this and from the "block and gap" plan in one important aspect. Rather than *following* the case or block, the student becomes involved in it. He must seek his own solutions.

One of the more successful uses of this approach is in the science course at Colgate University.[3] For example, the problem is posed, "Does the earth go around the sun, or the sun around the earth?" The answer at first seems obvious to the students. They have been told the correct answer from the time they were children. But, they have never looked at the evidence for themselves. When this is examined as it developed historically, and in the absence of refined modern scientific instruments, the answer is far less clear and the geocentric hypothesis becomes very tenable. The student, thus, comes to respect rather than ridicule the conclusions of his forbears who, on the basis of existing evidence, supported this hypothesis. He finds it not as easy as he thought to muster evidence supporting the reverse hypothesis which is more complex, less obvious, and requires refinements not available a few centuries ago. At this point history becomes meaningful.

Indeed, a skillful teacher can "weave a web" of uncertainty which will send his students to many sources in an effort to find evidence to restore certainty. Obviously, to use this method successfully requires a "gentleman's agreement" that reliance will be on evidence, not on authority.

The problem approach is used successfully in a number of areas of general education. In social science it may involve projects as well.

The Student-Centered Approach. In a sense this is not an approach. It is a philosophy related to the objectives of general education. The objectives of general education can be broken down in the first instance into two—the gaining of knowledge and understanding in the several areas common to a liberal education, and the development of awareness by the student of his own problems and his own environment. The two objectives are not incompatible, but the methods used by the teacher will depend in considerable measure on which of these claims priority in his mind. If it is the latter, he will be inclined to use a student-centered rather than a subject-centered approach.

The problems will, in this instance, be drawn largely from the students' own needs and experiences and be developed at a level where they can deal with them. The course will be structured quite largely according to the concerns of the students. It will often involve projects, both group and individual, and will have in it a good deal of non-directive or permissive atmosphere. Such courses usually include a good deal of independent or project work.

Obviously, this approach is particularly applicable in the social sciences, psychology, and personal adjustment courses. One of the most successful courses of this type in the social sciences was developed at Louisville University under the direction of Professor Robert Warner.[4]

While this approach is more usable in the social sciences than in other areas, it can be used in a somewhat modified way in both the natural sciences and the humanities. The Colgate science course already mentioned, while subject-centered, attempts to involve the student in the solution of problems in such a way that he is a participant, not merely an observer.

The distinction between the student- and the subject-centered approach is not as simple as it might seem. Indeed there are probably fewer courses which are clearly the one or the other than are courses which involve both to a considerable extent. And obviously, even if the principal objective involves a student-centered approach, we must still deal with subject matter.

The Use of Visual Aids. Visual aids can be and are used in many ways in education. They have no peculiar significance to general education. Indeed, the use of television in demonstrating surgical operations to replace the former gallery of student spectators is one of the most striking uses of this medium in education. It permits viewing of techniques impossible under the older method.

There are, however, many ways in which both films and television are important assets in the teaching of general education courses. We have, unfortunately, used films badly in many instances in the past largely because they were prepared for broad, general uses and we have not been sufficiently selective. In many instances *parts* of films should be used and *repeated*. Students need to be prepared, as in lectures, to look for certain emphases. Films prepared for general use often pass lightly over points needing more detailed attention in a course. They frequently cover more ground than is desirable for the purpose of the moment and they usually give the answers or conclusions which should be left to the students to provide. Finally, the actual physical arrangements of classrooms make films awkward to use. The class must be stopped, the shades pulled, the lights extinguished, and the projector started, usually by an operator other than the teacher. What is needed is an arrangement whereby the instructor can, without undue interruption, throw on the screen those parts of a film needed at the moment to illustrate a point. Such arrangements, hopefully, will soon be available.

Nevertheless, moving picture films can, when properly selected and used, contribute much to general education courses. We need more films and video tapes like "The Verdict is Yours," but without the jury's verdict, to use as cases without answers.

Television shows promise to make significant contributions to general education. It makes possible the use of large lecture-demonstration meetings in which the back row will see as well as the front row. With the use of video tapes, lectures and other important meetings can be repeated for those who missed the first meeting, or for emphasis or review.

Lecture and discussion can come in immediate sequence, as has been demonstrated at Stephens College where the lecturer speaks over a closed television circuit to several discussion groups in their separate classrooms. Immediately following the lecture the discussion leader in each room starts the discussion. Thus, there is no lapse of time; the group is of discussion size in familiar surroundings and with a leader they know. Discussion goes forward naturally in an atmosphere of informality. The discussion leader can, incidentally, use the occasion also to illustrate good note taking by outlining on the board as the lecturer proceeds.

There is little doubt that television will provide many more ways of increasing the effectiveness of teaching in general education, and many experiments are underway. It is too early, however, to know what new developments in the field may provide additional adjuncts to increase the effectiveness of teaching processes in general education. With educational networks well established around the country, the use of teaching talent from elsewhere and the development of video taped courses for use in many places become a real possibility.

Perhaps the most important point to be made in conclusion is that more experimentation in effective ways of teaching is greatly needed. We have but scratched the surface. In spite of the many centuries of teaching which are behind us, we still know little about how students learn and how teachers teach. Finally, teaching is an art, not a science. The important thing for each teacher is that he be willing to experiment to find out how he can be most effective, and that he be not satisfied to move along the path of least resistance—to lecture, good or bad.

We can take a lesson from Henry M. Wriston, President Emeritus of Brown University, and one of America's great educators, who reviews his own teaching experience in these words:

> The worst teaching I ever did was early in my career when I gave lectures to a class of three students. The best teaching I ever did was with upperclassmen to whom I never lectured, who never attended class. They worked independently, read widely and came to my study from time to time to submit their writing and discuss it, hear it criticized or praised, To make sure they had not over-specialized, they also took standard tests on subjects in which they had no formal instruction at all. Without a single exception they did well. To have sent them to hear a lecturer repeat what was available in books would have been a waste of their time and of my teaching energy.[5]

NOTES

[1] Clifton Fadiman, "Party of One," *Holiday,* October 1958.

[2] See Chapter X, "The Good Name of Science" by Eric M. Rogers, in *Accent on Teaching,* Sidney J. French, Ed. (New York, Harper & Brothers), 1954, for a description of this course.

[3] See Chapter VIII, "Physical Science: A Way of Thinking" by Clement L. Henshaw, in *Ibid.,* for a description of this course.

[4] See Chapter XIV, "Problems in Modern Society" by Robert M. Warner, in *Ibid.,* for a description of this course.

[5] Henry M. Wriston, "How the Colleges Can Handle the Throngs," *Life,* October 6, 1958, p. 140.

Chapter V

MATERIALS FOR TEACHING IN GENERAL EDUCATION COURSES

MARJORIE CARPENTER
Head, Division of the Humanities,
Stephens College

IN A real sense the best course materials are a professor full of fresh discoveries in his special field, and a student eager to capture the skills which will enable him to discuss ideas with his teacher. However, we usually mean by course materials the non-personal supplementary materials which enable the professor to make theories come alive for the student, and then provide the student with resources which make it possible for him to recapture the gains of the classroom and then go ahead on his own with new experiences which raise new questions.

SELECTION OF MATERIALS

Professor A meets his students at nine on Friday; he delivers a brilliant lecture, followed by a stimulating discussion, on "The Eighteenth Century, the Age of Enlightenment." What made it brilliant? What stimulated the discussion? His lecture was probably *not* a droning recitation, going on and on without any reference to source materials. His selection of sources depended first of all upon his objective. If his course is supposed to be a consideration of the various philosophic ideas men have held in the western world, he may have read to the students parts of Voltaire and parts of Rousseau; he may have thrown out questions which stimulated students to contrast the points of view expressed by these two writers. If, on the other hand, he wishes the students to understand the eighteenth century by examining man's creative expressions of his ideas, he would have to use materials not only from literature, such as Voltaire's "Candide," but he might also show a slide of Goya's painting "Maria Louisa of Parma," and compare it with Boucher's "Mme. Pompadour," and Chardin's "The Blessing." He might find it provocative to play a recording of a Bach Cantata, contrasting it to some of Gluck's "Orfeo" to illustrate the changes in thinking about music in the eighteenth century.

Here again, an even more careful examination of the objective is essential. Are the arts to be used merely to reveal eighteenth century culture, or are they to be understood for themselves, as a part of a process of increasing the student's aesthetic appreciation of music and painting? The answer to this question would, for example, determine the kind of emphasis to be placed on the music of Haydn. If music is to be understood for itself, Haydn's development of the symphonic form would be central; but Haydn would be useful in a quite different way if his late eighteenth century German music were to be compared with the early eighteenth century compositions of Scarlatti and Couperin to contrast the Italian, French, and German spirit in music.

Whatever the course objective, we shall assume that the teacher makes his selection of possible illustrative materials for his lecture with his main purpose in mind. He will also consider the materials which the student is to prepare on his own. The class demonstrations will be developed around the intention to help the student make his own applications. Between Friday at nine and Monday at nine, many things will have been happening to the student, and few of them will have had a direct relation to "The Eighteenth Century," although some may have contributed to a different sort of enlightenment! It will help in the on-going nature of the learning process if the student is expected to do some reading and exploring—either for a day's assignment or as part of a long term project. Obviously the direction for such assignments can be to many different types of materials: outlines, syllabi with readings attached, books of readings, manuals, textbooks, and outside resources, such as lectures or field trips.

OTHER CRITERIA FOR SELECTION OF MATERIALS

All of these various possibilities will be filtered through the teacher's own philosophy of education in general, his special objectives for his particular course, and his consideration of the size of the class, and the type of students who make up that class. Above all, if he is teaching a general education course, he will try to select those materials which broaden the student's point of view, and those which are relevant to live situations, with the best possible chance of proving significant not only at the moment but in the future life of the students. Ideally, the materials must provide for individual differences, and they must certainly be based on sound scholarship. It will heighten their effectiveness if references are made to a variety of subject matter, and if the student is asked to examine pairs of statements, pairs of pictures, pairs of musical compositions so that he is forced to think for himself about the principles under discussion.

It is at the point of selection of course materials that one of the chief characteristics of the general education course as distinct from the traditional liberal arts course becomes apparent. For the latter, there is usually the basic assumption that the students will go on with more highly specialized courses although some appeal to those taking the course for purposes of general background is planned. The reverse is true in the emphasis of the general education course. For example, in social studies a liberal arts course in American history may very well be taken by many students in order to improve their background in history; but the professor usually has in mind the materials which provide a more specialized information. The social science course which attempts to make available for the undergraduate an approach to current problems by making use of the various disciplines in this area will use quite different course materials.

TEXTBOOKS

Both may use a textbook. The American history professor will probably use a text. "A good text," says Dr. Geneva Drinkwater of Rollins College, "is one which contains the writer's comments in clear and readable form; and then has in a separate section the original sources on which he has drawn for his conclusions. The student and teacher need to have these sources within the covers of the one text." The type of source material used would naturally vary as one contrasts the highly specialized course and the one in general education. The latter might well have such material as Norman Cousins makes available in his book, *In God We Trust.*[1] In this collection, there are few detailed accounts of battles, there are few political documents; but the selection is slanted for the reader who wants an understanding of the philosophy which built this country, with an emphasis on the religious and ethical principles of our founding fathers.[2]

The text for the general education course will cut across the subject matter lines of history, economics, sociology, philosophy, geography, and the arts. It may focus around ideas through the centuries as does Crane Brinton's book, *The Shaping of the Modern Mind.*[3] In this book, source materials from literature and even references to the visual arts may be used by way of illustration. The arrangement of materials is appropriate to the objective since the historical ideas which have shaped the modern mind are to be central; but there is also an essential philosophic order which undergirds the text. Literature is important only as it heightens the concepts and the periods. "The Faustian Man" is important, for example, as a symbol of Humanism. Students read Goethe's *Faust* in order to comprehend Humanism as it is characterized by the excessive push for the satisfaction of infinite desires without any mediation of God. Supplementing the text, there is a use of syllabi and assigned readings which clarify the skeleton outline of the course and suggest both required and supplementary reading. For large classes and for individual differentiation, essays are suggested, such as "What do you find 'modern' in any *one* of the following: Erasmus, Rabelais, More?" or "Do you agree that the Humanists of the Renaissance had little effect on the development of democracy?" It is to be noticed that these essay questions attempt to relate historical concepts and outside reading to present day issues.

In the general science course at the University of Minnesota, a textbook is used.[4] Professor David Cooperman, who teaches the course, reports that for Part I in the section on personality he uses various outside readings in order to provide factual information and to offer some alternative points of view. In the chapter on the psychoanalytic view of personality, he makes use of the original lectures of Sigmund Freud. Other sections make similar use of original sources. Professor Cooperman also comments on the value of carefully chosen case studies to excite the student's imagination and illuminate theoretical points.[5] The use of case studies is common for courses in social science, science, and psychology.

A general education social science course at Drake University is taught by a team of four persons; the late Dr. Doyle Mikesell stated its chief objective as follows: "The student should become acquainted with significant problems in the social sciences and should be aware of their interrelated nature." This course makes use of a mimeographed syllabus which contains the course outline, a list of assignments, and reading materials not available in other tests and reference books. The student is asked to buy three books and assignments are made to ten others. Through the use of these various materials the instructor attempts to train the students to make a distinction between three approaches to the study of social science problems: theory, the formation of policy, and administration. Critical and analytical thinking are thus developed.[6]

OUTSIDE RESOURCES

There can be course materials which make a maximum use of outside resources and a minimum use of texts. At Sarah Lawrence College, Dr. Edward C. Solomon, Director of Field Work, writes that he has a teaching connection with about two-thirds of the students. He assists students with contracts which involve a collection of empirical data, he places them in community agencies in connection with their course work, involves them in community activities, and helps organize field observation trips. During the past year, in addition to many short trips such as visits to child development clinics, a few students went on a nine-day tour to Canada, and a two-week trip to Puerto Rico. Field work is used flexibly according to the interests and needs of the students; its major aim is the involvement of the student in her own education in a way related to her own experiences. Though used more heavily by courses in which human behavior is studied, some use of field work is found in practically every course.[7]

This type of course material is not appropriate to every college. It is in line with the philosophy of Sarah Lawrence to emphasize individualized programs and work; it is suited to a small student body, to the location of the college near New York, and to the clientele of women students coming from above the average economic groups.[8] This does not mean that such a course would not have a text.[9] It is useful for class purposes to have material to which all can refer, to have illustrations which are not easy to come by, and to have enough of them that students can be asked to make comparisons. Principles are available for reference, even though many teachers prefer to have students work out the principles for themselves and then find them summarized in black and white for review and future reference. No matter how well the text is organized, no matter how well the principles are clarified, the examples in the text do not provide the same kind of vital experiences, however, as those which the student can have from supplementary live performances.

The use of live drama as one kind of valuable course material will illustrate some of the points previously made about the criteria for selection of materials. For example, let us suppose that the college playhouse puts on a performance of Sartre's *The Flies.* The philosophic problem of man's responsibility for his own acts, and the philosophic doctrine of existentialism, are of both immediate and long term concern to the student; and there is no question about their power to stretch the student's thinking and provoke discussion. Sound scholarship must prepare the way by lecture or assignments in connection with the story of Orestes, the tenets of existentialism in general, and Sartre in particular. Infinite possibilities are apparent for development of projects of individual interest, such as assignments for study of all of the Greek dramas on the Orestes story, comparisons of dramatic treatment in all of the dramas studied, essays on personal philosophy, and essays on current French political problems. The variety of subject matter involved adds to the value, and all of these points serve to supplement the theoretical study of drama from text and lecture.

SELECTION WHICH AIMS AT MAXIMUM USE

It is important in general education courses to weed out the material which does not immediately serve the maximum number of objectives. This is often done at the expense of special pet units of the professor, and it requires single-mindedness of purpose. For example, what is to be done with architecture in a humanities course? Perhaps nothing. However, if the course aims at understanding cultural change, the presentation of historical styles is of great importance since buildings reflect very directly the way people live—the sort of buildings they want and the labor conditions which will produce them, to say nothing of the geographical limitations and the materials available. On the other hand, if the course centers in philosophy, it might be deemed wise to do more reading in original literary sources, and to pay little, if any, attention to architectural styles.

If the course tries to increase appreciation of the arts, the teacher will have some difficult decisions to make. Even though travel has made available to the teacher personal slides of such countries as Greece; and even though time might profitably and joyously be spent on a sort of travelogue interspersed with bits of archaeology, there is a real question as to the comparative value of this approach as against a *quick* survey of historical developments and a *lengthy* comparison of styles of *contemporary* houses and public buildings. The point is simple but difficult: which approach in a limited time will teach principles of judgment of style, and at the same time be of most concern to the student? The answer to that may well depend on the clientele of the student body. Film strips of historical styles can be shown as a quick background which precedes the showing of contemporary slides, and the reading about architecture today. Some students may well have actual building projects in mind for themselves and/or their families; for them it would be valuable to supply mimeographed bibliography, facts about costs (this has to be kept up to date), and even assignments which require the drawing of floor plans. Personally conducted trips which make possible study and criticism of local buildings or the architecture in a nearby town may well provide better course material than slides.

CREATIVE OPPORTUNITIES

Above all, the course which aims at an understanding and appreciative approach to the arts should provide many opportunities for the student to try his hand at some sort of creative work. Some teachers have made laboratory experience a required part of course materials;[10] others use it more flexibly and make it an optional assignment for different units. There is no question as to the stimulating effect produced by such treatment. For example, the class has read and seen a performance of Euripides' *Medea;* and they have been studying the principles involved in contemporary abstract painting. Suggest that they try first a presentation in lines and shapes which portray either the main mood of the play or of any scene in it. Then ask that this be designed in color. If the young artists do not label their attempts, and the class is asked to see first if the design is beautiful apart from the meaning, then if they know what the student was trying to say through line and color, a great deal of learning can be achieved. The experimenting artist is there to tell his fellow students whether or not they have understood his meaning; they are surprised at how much feeling is conveyed by line and color; and best of all, a few really good abstractions encourage some people to try to create in this medium.

Group creative efforts are rewarding. For example, a class has finished reading Sophocles' drama, *Antigone;* they have seen the later play by Anouilh. One student has come from Europe where the problems of the displaced person, the problem of the collaborator, are fresh; another student is from a professor's home in California where the moral difficulties connected with the oath of political allegiance were general topics of home conversation. Another student has ambitions to write for radio and still another is musical. In this particular class, the discussion centered on issues involved in independence as against collaboration with a ruler who believed he was doing his patriotic best. With this inspiration the radio student wrote a play centered around a California professor who refused to take the oath; the music student, who had come in with musical themes scored for Antigone and Creon, adapted them to the radio play, which was used locally. The principles involved in this example are, perhaps, self-evident; but they are worth repeating: use student interests *when* you recognize them, and stay alert for special abilities so that they can be called into play; in *practice,* inter-relate the arts whenever a natural opportunity for original creative work presents itself. Materials which have an immediacy teach theory better sometimes than prearranged formal treatment. In brief, the integration of materials from many subject matters, the individualization of assignments, the selection which has a chance at immediate and long term interests, have all been called into play. A by-product of this unit was the stimulus it provided for a student's recognition of his own values in relation to individual responsibility to the state.

UNUSUAL COURSE MATERIALS

Many professors have been experimenting with materials which not only teach their courses to advantage but which also tend to force the student to a critical examination of his pattern of values.

Boston University wished their students to obtain concrete

proof that the study of ethics had more than intellectual value. They wished to have the students, at the end of two years of exposure to the courses in the division of literature, art, and philosophy, work out practical solutions to ethical problems; and they believed that the student would profit from an opportunity to formulate his conclusions, communicate his insights to others, and become aware of the interrelationship and interdependence of value systems.[11] The materials chosen for this project were the texts of the following: Thomas More's *Utopia,* Plato's *Republic,* Francis Bacon's *New Atlantis,* Edward Bellamy's *Looking Backwards,* Aldous Huxley's *Brave New World,* George Orwell's *Animal Farm,* B. F. Skinner's *Walden Two,* and *The Quest for Utopia,* an anthology. These materials were chosen because they present various treatments, through the ages, of the issues of human relations, economics, political structure, the place of artistic activity, the impact of science, and educational policy, as well as physical arrangements for transportation and buildings. With the above objectives in mind, these materials provided not only good literary models, but also a stimulus for creative thinking and clear expression of personal and social values. The selection made no attempt to include all philosophic treatises on politics; it did not include, for example, Machiavelli's *The Prince, Das Kapital,* by Marx, Adam Smith's *The Wealth of Nations,* nor Thorstein Veblen's *The Theory of the Leisure Class.* Specialized books on community architecture by such authorities as Frank Lloyd Wright, Richard Neutra, and Le Corbusier were also omitted. Other omissions will be evident; but the selection was made with the idea of making possible enough reading for stimulus and not too much for the possibility of thinking out in groups an articulation of personal philosophy. To spend all of the allotted time on reading would not achieve the desired end. Time had to be planned for group working over of ideas, and personal assessment of interrelated values until articulation of opinions became possible.

LIMITATIONS OF TIME

Available time is an important factor in the selection of course materials. The Utopian experiment at Boston University used six weeks at the end of the first two years. Eastern Kentucky State College has in mind a similar objective. They require prospective graduates to identify and clarify the ideological content of our cultural heritage while the students relate specialized knowledge to their personal beliefs and patterns of behavior. They have placed their course at the end of four years. They face the challenge of a selection of materials with the following criteria in mind:

First, there should be a number of critiques consciously directed at values and beliefs current among our students. Paine's *Age of Reason*, Veblen's *Theory of the Leisure Class*, and Benedict's *Patterns of Culture* would fall under this head. Second, there should be a number of great works that present ideas and judgments in clear contradiction to those which most students hold. Plato's *Republic*, Simpson's *Meaning of Evolution*, and Freud's *A General Introduction to Psychoanalysis* are useful. Third, outstanding classics and works that deal with the perennial problems inevitably raised by an examinataion of beliefs and values must be included. Examples of such writers are Plato, Aristotle, Aquinas, Adam Smith, and Mill, as well as Descartes, Locke, Hume, and Kant. Finally, an attempt is made to give students an introduction into the works of those outstanding men whose thought today dominates perennial enquiries into the nature of thought and truth. Ayer, William James, and Langer are choices for the problem of knowledge and truth. Benedict, Lowith, and Tawney are considered useful in the area of the social sciences. Sullivan, and a book of the nature of Gardner's *Great Essays in Science* present good examinations of the problems of the natural sciences. Kant, James, Nietzsche, Kierkegaard, and Buber are selected as outstanding present day influences in the area of religion and ethics.[12]

This list of materials is longer because more time is available than the six-week unit at Boston University. It includes some more difficult material because it is offered at the end of four years and not two. It has some slightly different objectives, namely, the insistence on contradictory points of view. Significantly, the students call this course the "If" course because they are constantly expected to consider which values and beliefs they really hold and which they think they hold. Each student is challenged to become a reflective and intelligent person in his attempt to see what would happen *if* his opinions were followed out to their logical conclusions.

COURSE OUTLINES AND READING LISTS

A rather unusual combination of materials is appropriate for a course at the University of Michigan which sets out to meet four objectives:

A. To have the student examine his own and other religions in terms of psychological concepts and theories.

B. To show the use of the scientific method in approaching religion.

C. To state the relationship between psychological theory and research and the truth and adequacy of religion.

D. To have the student formulate his own religious view and examine it in the light of the ideas presented in the course.[13]

A course outline is put in the hands of the students so that they can follow the progress of lectures which deal with the interrelationship of the two subject matter fields of religion and psychology. The course is listed under psychology, but the readings in the course outline contain such books on religion as G. L. Berry, *Religions of the World,* William James, *The Varieties of Religious Experience,* J. B. Noss, *Man's Religions,* Ostow and Scharfstein, *The Need To Believe,* and Max Weber, *The Protestant Ethic.* Books on psychology are also included. In addition to the reading materials for the students, a number of other sources were used by the staff. Some of the more important of these were *Christian Paths to Self-Acceptance,* by R. H. Bonthius, *The Psychology of Religious Mysticism* by J. H. Leuba, *When Phophecy Fails,* by L. Festinger, H. W. Riecken, and S. Schachter, and *Changing Values in College* by Philip E. Jacob.

It is noteworthy that the materials used by the professor tend to emphasize religious experience as seen by psychologist and sociologist; whereas the student's reading is of a more factual nature. The students are, however, assigned to an unpublished monograph by Ronald Greene entitled "A Psychological Interpretation of Religion." This material was selected because it provided a survey of the relation between psychology and religion and a discussion of some of the major topics; it also provided a helpful bibliography. Since no single text was assigned in the course, the materials were on reading lists. This kind of approach to reading materials serves the purpose of placing responsibility on the student for the kind of reading which improves his discussion; and discussion is obviously extremely important for an objective which centers in the student's reexamination of the basis for his beliefs.

MATERIALS WHICH STIMULATE DISCUSSION

To supplement reading and to stimulate discussion, a different type of course material proved useful in this course at Michigan. Panel presentation of three religious points of view by a Catholic priest, an Episcopalian rector, and a Jewish director of student religious activities provided model statements by adults. Also, this approach tends to make a more vital impact; students react to people more than to printed words.

The possibility of incorporating the use of film into the plans for presentation of course material is demonstrated in this course by the use of a motion picture of the religious life of an Indian tribe. This emphasizes the place of religion in primitive cultures. In a subtle way it serves to focus the student's attention on the consideration of magic as distinct from religion, and tends to lead to the student's reexamination of his own beliefs.

ORIGINAL MATERIALS

It is traditional for the science teacher to use demonstrations and to supply students with manuals as supplements to textbooks, but Dr. John H. Woodburn of Johns Hopkins University worked out an original set of materials in order to emphasize the philosophical objectives inherent in general science courses.[14] First of all, he composed five brief descriptions of patterns of thinking which are identifiable in the history of civilization.

These statements are summaries of the way men react to natural science and formulate a philosophy which in turn gives the scientist a new consciousness of the principles which have been basic to his work. Three topics were chosen for consideration, namely, magnetism, heredity, and diastrophism with particular emphasis on earthquakes. Then passages were selected from historically significant discussions of these three phenomena; and these were duplicated and given students as instructional material for classroom use.

Teaching activities made use of the usual demonstration approach until students were familiar with the concepts, skills, and attitudes inherent in the investigation. At this point the stage was set for a discussion which posed such questions as: "What property of magnetism is identified by the demonstration?" "If you accepted theory A regarding the nature of magnetism, what would be your explanation of this property?" After each of several of the five theories were discussed, the students were ready for the final question: "Which of the following things is most important in determining the kind of theory that may be developed to explain such a phenomenon as magnetism? (1) The general pattern of thinking at the time. (2) The accuracy with which data can be observed. (3) The number of other theories that have been disproved."

The principle involved in this selection of materials is that the topics to be covered were few but the objective was difficult to attain: a critical and thoughtful recognition on the part of the student of the relationship between scientific method and philosophical theories. For such a purpose, the teacher had to create materials such as the brief descriptions of historical thought patterns, mimeographed passages of historically significant discussions of the three topics, and a set of questions. All of these supplement demonstrations and provide a new kind of laboratory. Perhaps we who teach need to remind ourselves that one of the course materials of the greatest importance is the careful selection of the questions to be posed after all the other materials have been presented.

MANUALS

The use of a laboratory manual for science courses is common practice. An interesting experiment has been conducted at the University of Minnesota in a course offered in the general college there. This course is directed toward the student who does not intend to take a typical preprofessional course in one of the biological fields, but wants to broaden his educational background in this area. The student is required to purchase a general text, and is given another reference text in the library. In addition to three lectures a week, he is required to attend a one-hour demonstration laboratory each week. Experiments are set up for the student to observe, and these experiments emphasize and extend the lecture materials. Also, a biology laboratory notebook is required of the students, who are asked to write answers or make drawings during the demonstration laboratory. A pilot study has been made of this approach. Sections were arranged so that one group took the demonstration laboratory, a second group completed a set of exercises in a biology workbook, and a third group wrote an eight to twelve page report on a topic of their choice. The demonstration lab group did significantly better work than the other two.[15]

Ottawa University has prepared a syllabus for their entire general education curriculum. In the general biology course, the student is given both a text and a laboratory manual. One of the objectives of this course is training in laboratory technique. In the general education course in physical science, on the other hand, seven problems are considered and an extensive bibliography is used for student reference. In the physical science course there is no laboratory training; the emphasis is on the development of logical reasoning.[16]

AUDIO VISUAL EQUIPMENT

Recent years have seen a remarkable development of the many aids supplementary to text and lecture. The basic principles of selection of good material still apply, and perhaps extra warnings are necessary so that variety and novelty do not become substitutes for essential presentation of material. It is of great advantage to appeal to as many of the senses as possible if learning is to take place with any degree of permanence and significance. The gadget without the consideration of purpose, without preparation and follow-up discussion, is, however, useless. Records, slides, reproductions of paintings, strip films have all been mentioned; turnover charts, tape recordings, and films need a special comment.

The blackboard can, of course, contain course materials which are of advantage in development of discussions. The key question, or the basic idea can be placed there in advance and students can be challenged to develop the proof or the subheads. Many times, this can be done still better by the use of a turn-over chart, which will structure the discussion and reveal only one idea at a time as the pages are flipped, with the main point on each side waiting to be filled out. It provides a way for inexpensive duplication of quotations or outlines which the student copies and even considers more carefully because he has to copy it. Students can be asked to draw examples or diagrams which heighten the principles; or students who conduct panel discussions can prepare their main points on the chart in professional fashion for presentation to each other.

Tape recordings make possible the reproduction at an appropriate time of the comments of a visiting lecturer. They serve also to reproduce the comments and the music which it would be difficult to assemble in compact form. Best of all, the recorded class discussion provides material for the students to hear themselves and evaluate their contributions. Playbacks of previous class material can serve as review or self-evaluation. (They also provide the teacher with humiliating evidence of his own tendency to talk too much.)

SELECTION OF FILMS

Films are wisely used as course material whenever discussion is stimulated by an objective presentation; for example, the film

Boundary Lines drives home the stupidity of interracial prejudice better because of the abstraction in such scenes as the lynching of a Negro; and it also serves to present quickly and forcibly the stupidity of weapons in different periods of culture. The disintegration of the body in the abstract design following the dropping of the atom bomb is a subtle reminder of the effects of atomic missiles in a total war.

Films are very valuable as course materials when processes are made clear. The making of a stained window glass, the steps in preparing lithographs or etchings, or the casting of bronze statues can be shown in economical fashion. The creation of works of art takes so long to observe that it is difficult to give students the direct experience. A similar service is rendered by the film on the Sadler's Wells Ballet. The steps of classical ballet are illustrated, and the process of putting together a ballet is made clear in a short space of time.

Also, an appreciation of the pains which the artist takes in the creation of a work of art can be conveyed in such a film as the one on Matisse, whereas lectures on the subject would leave the student unconvinced. Another important contribution of the film is the opportunity it affords for looking at the kind of art which is not easily available. The film, "French Tapestries Visit America," for example, shows in color masterpieces of tapestry which one could not see even on an extended tour of Europe. Films need to be selected with care; they must be fitted into the objectives of the unit being studied; the teacher must prepare for them and discuss the points made in them—otherwise, films can become substitutes for good instruction.

Films can then be of great importance as instructional materials either as the point of departure for good discussion, or as means for presenting painful issues in objective fashion, or as quick, clear descriptions in action of processes, or as a means of making available experiences which are rare but important.

TELEVISION

With the growth of television, new kinds of course material

are necessarily being developed. Leaving aside for the moment the advantages and disadvantages of presenting a course entirely over television,[17] the experiences of those who have used this medium point up the fact that it can be used for purposes other than that of trying to reduce the faculty teaching load. It is obviously a good medium for the kind of course which teaches method or skills or processes. How can it be used to meet the needs of general education courses in ideas? One example of an effective approach to all of the student body can be observed in the course called Ideas and Living Today which is now offered at Stephens College. All entering students take the course at the hour just before lunch. This time is important, since the discussions which start when the lecturer has stopped and go on through the rest of the class hour hopefully continue over the noonday meal. After a twenty-minute lecture given over television, various small groups with their leaders discuss the material.

Such an approach demands certain careful consideration of course material. First of all, the lecturer does well to use some visual material; but if it is brought in just to show off the new medium, or if it does not heighten the points made by the person who is talking, it defeats its purpose. It is possible to have the lecturer himself the point of visual interest. In this case, it does help if he changes position, if he talks and does not read. Too many gadgets shown too rapidly defeat their purpose. It is very important that students have outlines and mimeographed materials to help them remember what was said, since good notes are hardly possible in a darkened room if one is watching a television screen. It is helpful if the student is provided with small pictures which duplicate those shown by the lecturer in case close observation of pictures is a part of the follow up discussion. Wherever charts are used on the television screen, the class materials may well include either a duplication of the chart, or a skeleton which the student is asked to fill in. Suggested questions are of great value. In fact, almost all of the principles discussed and the suggestions made about course materials in the class room apply here. Films can be used, and panel discussions are excellent for stimulating discussion. The materials can be chosen from many subject matter areas to make clear the contribution of each discipline to current issues.[18]

The principles which must be borne in mind if a general education course is to be successful in its selection of materials are inherent in the characteristics of such courses as distinct from more specialized traditional courses. The fact that integrated material of breadth of interest is to be presented so that it affects a substantial part of the student body and at the same time provides for individualization, and the fact that its aims can be stated in terms of human behavior and that these goals are viewed as intrinsic and not merely preparatory for advanced work—all of these considerations impose certain criteria for selection which complicate the work of the scholar and teacher. He must, even to a greater degree than usual, be clear about his main objective and work out certain interesting bypaths; he must choose assignment material which provides for various student interests even while it drives home central principles; he has to consider available time and realize that he can do well a limited number of things; he has to be original in adapting various devices and many resources to the needs of the group of students he teaches.

The demands of this careful selection of course material can produce richer teaching because the instructor himself has to grow, and to think creatively; he is forced to consider the interrelationship of facts from many areas and their significance for live issues.

NOTES

[1] New York, Harper & Brothers, 1958.

[2] A still more narrowly selected series is that by Vrooman, Lee, *The Faith That Built America* (New York, Arrowhead Books, Inc.), 1955.

[3] This is used as a text, for example, at Michigan State University, in a general humanities course. (New York: Prentice-Hall, 1950.)

[4] Ross, Ralph and Van den Haag, Ernest, *The Fabric of Society* (New York, Harcourt, Brace and Co.), 1957.

[5] From a letter in which Professor Cooperman explains in detail the use of supplementary materials.

[6] From a letter written by Dr. Doyle Mikesell, June 1958.

[7] From a letter written June 11, 1958.

[8] A detailed account of the way in which field work is made an integral part of the curriculum at Sarah Lawrence College is given in Lynd, Helen Merrel, *Field Work in College Education* (New York, Columbia University Press), 1945.

[9] It is worthwhile examining the preface to *The Humanities* by Dudley and Faricy (New York, McGraw-Hill Book Co.), 1951 to read the clear statement of the difference between a general education course and the more traditional course: "In content, this study of humanities differs from the traditional approaches in three major ways: First, it approaches the arts through their common principles, subject, medium, function, elements, organization, and style. Second, it tries to supply the vocabulary and equipment by which any individual can make his own criticism, his own analysis, and realize his own appreciation. Third, and most important, this approach uses the work of art as the beginning and end of the study." Details are given in this preface of various principles of organization and selection of materials which demonstrate the need for the writers of texts to choose materials with great care in the light of the special aims of the course.

[10] The University of Chicago originally required laboratory work for the beginning course in humanities.

[11] This experiment was described in "Education for Citizenship," by James Fisher and Peyton Richter, in *Journal of Higher Education,* April 1957, pp. 220–224.

[12] The course is officially called "Ideological Foundations of Western Civilization." Kerney M. Adams and James R. Flynn have described their criteria of selection in an unpublished paper which they made available to me for an analyst's presentation at the meeting of the Association for Higher Education in the Chicago meeting in March 1958.

[13] William J. McKeachie prepared a paper on "The Psychology and Religion Course at the University of Michigan" for me to use as analyst at the meeting of the Association for Higher Education in March 1958. These statements are taken from his paper.

[14] The substance of what is said here is abstracted from an unpublished paper by Dr. Woodburn.

[15] Abstracted from a letter written by Professor Douglas M. Dearden who was good enough to send a copy of the laboratory notebook for the course in Human Biology, along with the mimeographed workbook and the directions for the biology report.

[16] Ottawa University General Education Syllabus, 1957–58 (mimeographed).

[17] Quotations from six papers presented at the March 1958 meeting of the Association for Higher Education will summarize some of the main points. These papers will later be incorporated into *Current Issues of Higher Education, 1958.* Washington, Association for Higher Education, 1958.

"Classrooms and lecture halls have some advantage over television, particularly for teachers who employ the Socratic method. On the other hand, television offers advantages, particularly for teachers who are clear expositors. . . . Television should be compared, not with an idealized situation, but with the feasible alternatives." Holbrook M. MacNeille, Group 20.

"Without the help of great professional direction, educational television will never realize its full potential. . . . Good teachers only should be chosen; the teacher should have time for preparation; the teacher should be given the help of a person who knows television production. . . . The director forces the teacher to pound ideas into clarity, economy, and relevance." John Colby Lewis, Group 20.

"The real academic dangers are: loss of direct contact between student and instructor, increase of passivity on the part of the student, standardization of content and teacher." H. Burr Roney, Group 20.

"The teaching environment of a studio is not likely to produce any original ideas, but it is an adequate setting for communicating knowledge." Francis A. Gaul, Group 21.

"Evaluation shows that there is no significant difference between televised and direct instruction—the evidence that university teaching can be improved by television is not yet very encouraging—student acceptance of televised instruction is economically feasible." Leslie Greenhill, Group 21.

"If (as has been demonstrated) students can learn by television, we should use it to curtail the rise in per pupil cost of instruction, and as a way of meeting deterioration in instruction by the shortage of teachers." J. Paul Leonard, Group 21.

[18] For example, the following issues will be discussed in the series in 1958–1959: Education: liberal and special; Tradition and Change; Similarity and Diversity; Dogmatism and Skepticism; Expediency and Principle; Freedom and Authority; The Right and Acceptable. In each group there are individual presentations by teachers from various disciplines; after four or five individual lectures, a panel is used to focus attention on different points of view and different emphases in the various disciplines. Students, by this method, are stimulated to discuss both new approaches and their own points of view.

Chapter VI

DEVELOPING THE GENERAL EDUCATION FACULTY

B. LAMAR JOHNSON
JAMES L. McKENNEY
University of California, Los Angeles

PRACTICES reported in other chapters—including those dealing with administration, curriculum, teaching, student personnel, and evaluation—inevitably contribute to faculty development. Similarly, effective administration, curriculum, teaching, student personnel, and evaluation are in large measure dependent upon staff improvement. The present chapter is, therefore, directly related to materials presented in other parts of this volume. The emphasis here, however, is upon the contributions which the programs and activities reported make to the personal and professional growth of faculty members.

Writers repeatedly emphasize the importance of faculty improvement to curriculum development. Antell for example asserts ". . . curriculum method is synonymous with teacher growth and coterminous with it."[1]

Carlin goes so far as to state that "without exception where programs of general education are distinguished there can be found active, interesting, and well-planned programs of in-service training."[2]

As a basis for writing this chapter, correspondence was carried on with leaders in the field of general education, with foundation executives, and with professors of higher education for the purpose of identifying colleges and universities which give particular attention to faculty development. The literature of general education and of staff improvement was also reviewed as an aid to locating institutions which have effective plans, as well as to learn of specific practices which are reported to be successful.

Letters of inquiry were subsequently sent to administrators of more than fifty colleges and universities, raising the following questions:

1. What practices do you use which, in your judgment, contribute most effectively to the development of your faculty in general education?

2. What additional practices which you do not use would you like to follow (or perhaps plan to follow in the future) as an aid to staff development?

3. What practices have you found to be ineffective and would you therefore advise other colleges not to use?

This chapter describes practices which colleges and universities—through correspondence, published materials, and unpublished documents—report contribute to faculty development. Some attention will also be given to additional plans which administrators would like to use, as well as to some activities which have not been successful. Although emphasis is given to practices in institutions with established curricula in general education, plans are also reported from institutions whose programs do not answer the criteria suggested by Mayhew in Chapter I if, in the judgment of the authors, these procedures are adaptable for use in programs for general education.

In describing practices, no attempt has been made to classify plans according to the type or size of the institution. Some procedures reported by the University of Minnesota, a huge and complex university, may perhaps be suggestive for Goucher College—and *vice versa*. Likewise, a plan used at Wright Junior College may have relevance for Carleton College or the University of Florida.

Activities which contribute to faculty development will be reported under two headings: 1) practices planned specifically for their value to staff improvement, and 2) those carried on primarily for purposes of institutional development, but which also contribute to faculty growth. It is clear, of course, that the specific intent of a given plan may be difficult to identify. Some practices are planned for both faculty and institutional improvement. The authors have, therefore, used their own discretion in classifying plans whose purposes are not completely clear or are dual in nature.

I. PRACTICES PLANNED FOR THE PURPOSE OF FACULTY DEVELOPMENT

Faculty development programs, as conceived here, aim to assist instructors to broaden their horizons and experiences, attack individual teaching problems, achieve an orientation to the college and its program, evaluate themselves, and strengthen their work.

Faculty Seminars. Several colleges use seminars or study groups, in some cases made possible by foundation grants, in their programs of faculty development.

Carleton College has held summer seminars especially for new instructors. In 1956, for example, a six-week seminar was arranged for eight new members of the faculty. In preparation for their study the group met weekly during the spring semester, under the chairmanship of a professor of English, for discussions of classroom procedures, the psychology of learning, and the history and philosophy of higher education. These sessions were also used for planning the summer seminar, at which it was agreed that each instructor would present to his colleagues a course which he was to teach for the first time the following fall. The procedure and spirit of the group during the summer session are suggested by the following description:

> The person who was to lead the meetings, for example the philosopher, would open with a lecture analysis of the material which he had assigned to the members of the seminar. The lecture would last for thirty or forty minutes and then discussion would begin. The discussion ranged in its subject matter from the philosophic implications of Free Will to

semantic quibbling, from major questions of educational philosophy to minor points of teaching techniques. After thirty or forty minutes of discussion, we usually took a coffee break in the library's kitchen-lounge. Here the discussion was continued; new and oftentimes devious side roads were explored. We then returned to the seminar room and the lecturer gave the group some specific problems to solve and discuss. For example, our philosopher gave us three or four problems and then discussed the various ways such problems could best be presented to a class of undergraduates. The meetings would usually adjourn after three hours, and we spent the afternoons preparing our assignments for the next member of the seminar who was to hold forth on the following day.

In this manner each member of the seminar presented three different aspects of his course and discussed his examinations during the course of another meeting. He had ample time (eight days) to prepare for each of his sessions, and in the meantime had done a goodly amount of reading in the disciplines of all the other participants.[3]

Members of the Carleton group appraise the values of their seminar, in part, as follows:

There is an almost startling unanimity among the members of the seminar on the values of the summer program. All felt that the combination of a subject matter with teaching and discussion of teaching proved highly rewarding. . . .

A second gain from the seminar was the renewed or new feeling of being a member of a community of scholars. This was stated by every member of the seminar, and it was emphasized by many that this was the first occasion on which the effects of graduate school compartmentalization were dispelled or at least made innocuous. A number of reports remarked that this was the first time that the unity of the college became apparent.[4]

In contrast with the evaluation of the summer seminar is the appraisal of the weekly meetings held during the spring semester:

Most felt that the spring session devoted to discussions of teaching in the abstract were useless. Discussion of the reports and books on liberal education were frequently commented on negatively although some felt they served a useful purpose in preparation for the latter part of the seminar.[5]

Hunter College reports on seminars held during the college year for twelve junior (not more than three years of teaching) and eight senior members of the faculty. Before the fall semester opened, a two-day orientation session was held and during the year there were twenty-four two-hour meetings at which such topics as these were studied: "What Are the Major Purposes of the Good College Teacher?" "Planning a Course," "Teaching by Discussion," "Evaluation of College Instruction," "Trends in General Education," and "General Education at Hunter College." In order to provide time for preparation and participation in seminars junior and senior members were given, respectively, 40 per cent and 20 per cent reductions in their teaching loads.

> Seminar presentation varied from week to week. For some meetings, outside consultants were called in from other departments of the college and from other institutions. Sometimes a member of the seminar led the discussion; sometimes panels of visitors or of seminar members took charge. . . .
>
> A rating sheet at the end of each seminar gave an opportunity for the group to evaluate each meeting. . . . The weekly rating sheets have indicated how useful members of the seminar found particular meetings. Among other things, they have revealed that the desires and interests of the senior members of the group are sometimes quite different from those of the junior members.[6]

Although participants "testify to increased awareness of teaching problems . . . and a broadened knowledge and interest in the problems of higher education,"[7] the values of the seminar were, it appears, somewhat limited:

> Perhaps one can only speculate about the reasons for the limitations on the success of the seminar. The most obvious explanation seems to be that the seminar has concerned itself with problems or topics thought to be important by senior members of the seminar who assumed major responsibility for planning it, and that interests of primary importance to them are not always of equal importance to junior members. . . .
>
> If the incidental values of mixed membership, (that is, both junior and senior members of the faculty) are to be retained in such a program, and there is unanimous agreement that they should be, senior members

ought to impose severe restrictions on themselves both in planning and in participation in seminar discussions.[8]

At St. John's College the entire faculty participates in staff seminars. "We . . . deem it important," writes President Weigle, "that the faculty as a whole should be challenged by new ideas and should have a sense of oneness. To accomplish this we hold faculty seminars every three to five weeks. The reading in preparation for these seminars is determined by the faculty and the Instruction Committee. Sometimes new materials and new books are explored perhaps with a view to their ultimate inclusion in the curriculum. In other cases the faculty as a whole seeks new insights into books which are already a part of the curriculum."[9]

St. Johns also has a "Faculty Study Group,"

> . . . which normally involves from three to five faculty members each year. Members of this group are relieved of one-third of their teaching schedule to permit their full participation in the study group. In the first year of its operation the group studied both traditional and modern symbolic logic. During the present year poetics has been the subject for study and in the year to come the group plans to become involved in genetics. On occasion outside scholars are brought in to lecture to the entire college community and to meet with the Faculty Study Group for a period of two or three days. This group has proved a tremendous stimulus to the faculty and I am sure has broadened the outlook and the interest of the members participating.[10]

Quite different from those thus far reported is the "voluntary faculty seminar" at Kansas State Teachers College, Pittsburgh. Planned particularly for the study of general education, the seminar has an average attendance of thirty. Dean Ernest Mahan, who refers to this plan as "the most effective practice we have used for the development of our faculty in general education," particularly emphasizes voluntary participation. "Voluntary attendance seems to bring a noticeably stronger motivation than required attendance because of a sense of duty."[11]

A number of institutions use study groups to aid in the orientation of new faculty members. At Amherst College and at Brown

University, seminars which were initiated as parts of Internship Programs of the Fund for the Advancement of Education have been continued. Commenting on this plan, former Dean K. Ronald Bergethon of Brown University points out some of the difficulties associated with involving full-time faculty members in regular study sessions:

Some of the benefits from the Intern Program were transferable. On the whole, however, full-time instructors and assistant professors were not as anxious to learn as were the interns; they did not attend meetings of the Seminar as regularly; their over-all interest level was lower; and they showed little concern for topics which were not immediately applicable to their teaching or to their professional status.[12]

At Columbia College a teaching seminar for new instructors has been held for several years. "This seminar, run by two senior members of the faculty, meets every other week for two hours and is designed to supply the new instructors with information about Columbia, its educational philosophy, and its student body, and to give the new men an opportunity to discuss problems of mutual interest. It has been well received."[13]

The General College at the University of Minnesota holds five seminars early in the fall for all new staff plus any staff who have not previously been through the program. At these sessions the following subjects are considered: 1) General Education; 2) Objectives, organization and operation of the General College; 3) Counseling in the General College; 4) Teaching in the General College; and 5) The General College Comprehensive Examination.[14]

Faculty Meetings. Somewhat similar to seminars are faculty meetings planned as aids to staff development. Goshen College, for example, holds special faculty discussion meetings at which no business is conducted:

. . . we have found helpful . . . the use of special faculty discussion meetings. One meeting each month (usually a total of eight in the year) is devoted to a discussion session. At this time no business is transacted, but a faculty member or sometimes two faculty members make a report to the faculty as a whole on some controversial issue with respect to the content of general education. The entire faculty is then invited to participate in the discussion which follows.[15]

At the Basic College of Michigan State University, college-wide staff meetings are also held for purposes of staff development:

A . . . program that has proved quite successful for us has been the series of Basic College Colloquia that have been in progress during the past two years. The focal point of these colloquia has been the broad subject matter upon which the curriculum of the college rests. They have consisted for the most part of the . . . reading of papers and discussion followed by an informal social hour.[16]

Much like the Michigan State colloquia are the meetings of the basic studies faculty at Western Michigan University. Held on selected Friday afternoons, these sessions are devoted to explanations and descriptions of various courses by panels of those who teach them. In commenting on the values of these meetings, Robert Limpus, the Director of Basic Studies, points out that "these general meetings must have been informative and useful, or people would not have turned out on Friday afternoons to attend them."[17]

At Friends University monthly meetings of the Faculty Club have recently been concerned with the development of effective college teachers. One outcome of these meetings has been a survey during which "students were asked to list specific incidents from various classes which indicated in their estimation either effective or ineffective teaching."[18] The findings of this survey were used "as partial guidance in determining the direction our faculty study on the improvement of teaching might take. That these student opinions did influence us somewhat is apparent in the fact that two of the three areas which we selected for study were teaching by the discussion method and individualizing instruction, both of which ranked high in the students' comments."[19]

Individual Assistance. Plans described up to this point have involved groups of staff members—in seminars and study groups, in faculty meetings and colloquia. Most every college also, however, stresses work with, and assistance to, individual faculty members, particularly new instructors.

At Kansas State College, course chairmen "work individually with staff members"[20] and at Colorado State College work that individual division chairmen do with new faculty members is referred to as a "most effective practice."[21]

An experienced member of the faculty is assigned as adviser to each new faculty member at Sarah Lawrence College and in the College of General Education at Boston University. In commenting on this plan, former President Harold Taylor of Sarah Lawrence College asserts, ". . . we find that this is the key to most of the in-service training that is needed. . . . In general, I feel that the empirical approach is best, that is to say by having the new faculty member confer with his experienced colleagues on content of courses, on teaching methods, on college structure, on educational policy."[22]

A few reports give examples of specific types of individual work done with instructors. At Florida State University, a senior member of the faculty worked with an instructor of a general education science course whose teaching was ineffective. In particular, the young teacher was advised to visit classes of several colleges as an aid to improving his own teaching.[23]

From Antioch College comes a report of the special attention given to individual faculty members through the dean's review with them of criticisms received from student evaluations. Former President Gould observes, "These student evaluations can be so handled as to be damaging to good teaching; but if properly used, they provide the Dean with a most helpful occasion for counseling with the teacher and may also give specific clues as to his major teaching problems. College criticism should be included."[24]

Amherst College has carried over from its Ford Internship Program a plan under which "a young teacher may ask an experienced teacher to visit his class and criticize his teaching. Just this year, we have arranged to make tape recordings of any class, if the teacher wishes one. These are solely for his own personal use so that he may hear himself lecture, leading a discussion, etc."[25]

Encouraging Advanced Study. Additional graduate or post-doctoral study is encouraged at a number of institutions. The College of St. Catherine grants and encourages "leaves of absence for study in fields of general education."[26]

At Colgate University, grants from the Ford Foundation have made it possible for faculty members who teach general education courses "to improve their knowledge by visiting and studying at other institutions. . . ."[27] Colgate in addition recognizes the value of supplementary study in courses on its own campus: "In a few instances members of core course staffs have been given substantial release from departmental duties in order to audit courses in other departments."[28]

Varied Assignment of Teaching Responsibilities. Some colleges assign staff members to the courses they are to teach in such a way as to contribute to faculty development. At Chatham College, for example, faculty participation in teaching a variety of general education courses is encouraged. In explaining this practice President Paul R. Anderson comments, "Where possible we rotate teaching responsibilities in these interdepartmental courses in order that the largest possible number of faculty members may have both interest in and support of the courses concerned."[29]

At the College of the University of Chicago, instructors upon occasion teach general education courses in more than one division, as well as participate in inter-division courses:

In order to increase understanding and communications between the various staffs teaching our general courses, we have tried to provide for an inter-change of staff members. Instructors in our English (writing) course also teach sections of our general humanities courses. We have frequently found it possible to have the same person teach courses in both the social sciences and the humanities. Two of our general courses which are intended to integrate the student's education—a course in philosophy called Organizations, Methods, and Principles of Knowledge, and a course in the History of Western Civilization—have staffs made up wholly, or almost wholly, of persons who are primarily members of the College staffs in English, the Humanities, the Social Sciences, and the Natural Sciences. . . . Through experience in teaching in several courses within an area, and through experience in teaching courses in other areas, we feel that each faculty member gains the feeling that he is engaged in a common enterprise much larger than the area of his particular interest. This practice has made each staff aware of the problems of other staffs and of the problems of our whole program of general studies.[30]

A variety of practices planned for purposes of staff development have been reported: faculty seminars, faculty meetings, individual assistance, encouraging advanced study, and varied assignments of teaching responsibilities. Although these plans are in some instances directly relevant to program improvement, they largely focus upon staff members, their interests, their concerns, and their personal and professional growth.

Also important in staff development is their involvement in solving institutional problems and in working on education programs. In describing plans for faculty development, many administrators stress staff participation in improving the college and its offerings. This is what Spears had in mind when he asserted that "the story of in-service education is crossed with the story of curriculum development."[31]

2. PRACTICES PLANNED FOR PURPOSES OF INSTIUTIONAL DEVELOPMENT

At Michigan State University, much of the "in-service training has been associated with the formal departmental efforts at curriculum development and research. The virtue of this kind of operation is that members of the department have a common point of focus that in considerable measure reduces the insecurities and resentments that quite frequently accompany in-service training programs defined as such."[32]

In discussing faculty development at San Francisco State College, Joseph Axelrod refers particularly to the early history of general education at that college when "course staffs came into existence, the members of which were all teaching the same course, helping in its continuous planning and revision, making common decisions about texts, etc., and engaging in a very lively exchange of insights about modes of organizing and teaching the materials in that particular broad area. During this early period . . . it was hardly necessary to make efforts in the direction of in-service training. The staffs were doing that job as a very necessary part of the process of developing the courses and coming to feel at home with them."[33]

After general education courses have become well established, however, Axelrod points out that "distinct efforts had to be made if the various . . . staffs were to continue as entities, accomplishing the tasks of mutual education of members."[34]

Participation in Teaching. Some colleges point out that the participation of faculty members in the regular instructional program of the college contributes to both institutional and individual development.

This viewpoint is supported by Peyton Richter who asserts that "the main problem of faculty development . . . is the provision of a teaching situation in which the intrinsic personal rewards are felt on the part of the faculty member. He grows not because he *has* to do so, in order to be secure in his job, but because growth comes naturally as he is stimulated and nurtured in an environment conducive to growth."[35]

Dean William Perry of the General College of Boston University further supports this position. "I think what contributes most to the faculty member's development in general education is the attitude which the new man finds in the college, that his responsibilities are broad, that his own education is expected to be as broad as his responsibilities."[36]

President Weigle suggests the presence of a stimulating teaching environment at St. John's College which:

has, as one of its basic tenets, a conviction that faculty members should continue to educate and broaden themselves rather than specialize in a relatively narrow field. . . .

The heart of the St. John's program is seminar reading and discussion of a representative list of books throughout the four years. These books are drawn from the fields of literature, philosophy, history, religion, psychology, economics, and science. Tutors, therefore, often find themselves involved with a book which may be considerably outside of their special competence.[37]

Similarly, former President Taylor of Sarah Lawrence College notes the values which faculty members achieve through their regular teaching at that college ". . . since our total approach to teaching involves the use of the conference method, seminars and discussions, student and faculty committees on educational policy, empirical case studies dealt with by our Committee on Student Work. . . ."[38]

An unusual plan of institutional organization, and one which is directly related to faculty improvement, is followed at Boston University Junior College where students concurrently take five required general education courses. Each instructor is a member of a five-man team (one representative from each course) which throughout the year teaches—in five sections—the total program of from 125 to 150 students. Three members of each team share a common office, and the entire team meets weekly for discussions of teaching and curriculum but particularly of the students with whom they are working. Although the team is primarily an instructional and counseling unit, faculty development is a normal and necessary outcome. Richter asserts:

During the six years in which the team system has been used . . . it seems to have contributed in several ways to the growth and development of the faculty. . . .

It has aided each faculty member to see himself, his students and his discipline from a multi-dimensional point of view. . . .

Sharing the burdens and responsibilities involved in a collective coordinated faculty effort, each teacher avoids the dangers of academic provinciality. . . .

Continuing discussions among team members . . . often has provided incentives to teachers to continue graduate or post-doctoral research, sometimes in a field other than their specialty.

. . . these ways in which the team system furthers faculty growth and development are, I think, intrinsic modes of development as contrasted with the more externalized modes of development usually associated with a teacher's progress.[39]

The results of faculty associations in their day-to-day work are singled out for comment by Dean Carlin of Michigan State University who refers to

> . . . the informal type of experience that has been the concomitant of having in a single department a number of persons whose formal education has been in a number of different but related disciplines. For example, a humanities department of 35 members composed of persons who have taken their degrees in history, philosophy, theology, architecture, political science, and sociology are officed together. This creates a situation where a considerable exchange of information and ideas relative either to course content or teaching methodology is facilitated. I cannot over-emphasize the importance of this type of informal in-service training.[40]

Staff Meetings. Staff meetings—often teachers of single courses, at other times members of given departments or divisions—are repeatedly referred to as essential to the improvement of instruction and to curriculum development, and incidentally, to faculty growth.

At Drake University, for example, regular weekly meetings of area committees are held; at Amherst the staffs of large required courses meet weekly or semi-weekly.

The staff meeting is usually convened by the area or course chairman for the purpose of discussing specific problems of curriculum revision or teaching. It would appear from the correspondence that such a meeting serves as an incubator for ideas and a clearing house for faculty plans and projects.

The staff of each general education course at Colgate University meets regularly, usually weekly, for two hours. "It is common practice for the director to designate one member to lead off the discussion at each weekly meeting. Thus, for example, in our core course in Philosophy and Religion the Professor in Bible will lead the discussion on the Gospel of Mark or the Professor of Greek philosophy will lead the discussion on Plato and Aristotle. In this way we educate each other."[41]

At Kansas State College, "the chief device for in-service training is the staff meeting, which is generally held weekly. At these meetings the lectures and reading materials for the coming week are outlined, methods of approach in the classroom discussed, and special points of interest elaborated upon, argued, etc. . . . Revision of course organization and syllabi, discussion of examination questions and examination results, and the like, are other topics which engage staff members in such meetings."[42]

At Harvard University the value of staff meetings for younger members of the faculty is particularly noted: ". . . The practice of holding regular staff meetings for the young teachers and the head of the individual course is probably the most effective method we have found for giving beginning teachers or relatively inexperienced teachers the kind of guidance they need."[43]

Staff meetings with a particular purpose, and with faculty time released for participation, have been held at Colgate University for "instructors engaged in the development of a new sequence of courses in area studies, American Ideals and Institutions and in America in the World Community. Some members of this staff have been released from as much as one-half of their teaching duties for an entire semester for preparing themselves in teaching this course."[44]

Summer Workshops. In describing practices which contribute to staff development, several colleges refer to summer workshops during which faculty members are employed to work on curriculum planning, evaluation, or some other aspect of their work or of the college program. Salient points of successful workshops appear to be the solution of problems that are of concern and interest to faculty participants, adequate planning before sessions begin, financial compensation of those who attend, and a sufficient amount of time to work on the problem or development under study.

In the summer of 1957 Antioch College held a workshop at which, in preparation for the inauguration of its new general education program, plans were made for new courses and the revision of existing ones. The values of the workshop, not only for curriculum planning, but also for faculty development is suggested by this comment by a participant:

> In such a school as this, where it is socially acceptable to be interested in teaching, this kind of workshop might be the way to train college teachers with a maximum of involvement and a minimum of embarrassment. The experience of thinking through one's teaching aims and finding ways to reach them probably is about the most basic training one can have.[45]

Orange Coast College holds a series of workshops each summer. Faculty members are encouraged to submit proposals of problems and projects which they believe to be important and on which they would like to work during the summer. Following approval of a proposal by the administration, members of the workshop during the spring semester hold planning sessions to prepare for their summer work. Illustrative of plans followed at Orange Coast College is the 1956 two-week "Workshop in English" during which the objectives, content, and methods of introductory English courses at the college were studied by a group of eight instructors, including three new faculty members.

> Members of the workshop were unanimous in their feeling that the opportunity to discuss their common instructional problems in an atmosphere free of the pressure of class preparations and papers was very valuable: It enabled the faculty to achieve a common understanding of procedures and purposes that must result in improved instruction. The newer instructors were especially convinced that their induction to Orange Coast College would be smoother and more efficient as a result of this cooperative effort.[46]

At Goshen College in 1958 a three-week all-faculty workshop was held for the purpose of entering into "a common search for a deeper understanding of the Christian Faith and its implications for liberal arts education at Goshen College." Financed by the Libby Foundation, with all participants paid their regular sal-

aries, the workshop was regarded as "a new device for our study of our general education program. . . ."[47]

In addition to summer workshops held by individual colleges, representatives of groups of institutions at times participate in summer study projects.

The North Central Association Study on Liberal Arts Education describes the workshops which it sponsors each summer as follows:

> Each summer two workshops are conducted, each of four weeks duration. The one at the University of Minnesota is traditionally held in late June and early July while the one at Michigan State University is held in August. These conferences provide leadership, resources and leisure necessary for college teachers to concentrate on some problem of higher education of concern to them and their institution. They also provide the means by which participants can consider the problems of education more broadly than is possible under the stress of full work schedules during the academic year.[48]

Sister M. Verona LaBud, of the College of St. Scholastica in Duluth, Minnesota, comments on the value of these workshops:

> Since 1941, the North Central Association has conducted a program under its Liberal Arts Study Committee to encourage member colleges to achieve beyond mere accreditation limits. Part of this program includes the annual summer workshop where delegates from the various member institutions orient themselves to the idea and preferably work out some plan of action for which they will aim back home on their respective campuses during the following year. St. Scholastica has been in on this study since the beginning in 1941—a proud 17-year record.[49]

At the College of St. Scholastica, summer workshop representatives ordinarily coordinate and provide leadership in programs of college improvement (including planning general education courses, follow-up studies, institutional surveys) and concurrently of faculty development.

St. John's University, Collegeville, Minnesota, reports a plan under which representatives of three neighboring colleges (College of St. Benedict and St. Cloud State College, in addition to

St. John's University) have worked together in planning a Great Issues Course, enrollment in which will be limited to ten selected honor students from each institution. In connection with this course a program of faculty improvement is recommended by the planning committee—this program to include cooperative committee work, visiting consultants, summer study, and program appraisal.[50]

Pre-college Faculty Conferences. A considerable number of colleges hold faculty conferences just preceding the opening of the college year. Varying from one or two days to one or two weeks in length, such conferences involve all faculty members and are typically concerned with such matters as curriculum development, student personnel, improvement of instruction, institutional studies, issues in higher education, and staff orientation. Although sessions are usually held on campus, conferences in some cases are scheduled away from the college environment. At Goshen College, for example, where the annual faculty retreat is reported to be "very helpful," "The faculty leave the campus for a period of about 3 or 4 days just prior to the beginning of the fall semester and spend a part of the time in recreation and a part in various types of institutional studies."[51]

Stephens College has been holding pre-college faculty conferences, each from one to two weeks in length, continuously since 1921. In describing plans followed at the Stephens conferences Hugh McCammon states:

> The typical conference includes four kinds of experience. In certain 1) *general sessions* the president, guest consultants, and members of the administrative and teaching forces outline important policies, present facts and ideas from current educational theory and practice, or sketch problems for faculty consideration. In 2) *smaller group meetings* during each day of the conference, faculty members seek insight to the real and significant problems which they face, and solutions for them. Many of the groups so engaged cut across departmental lines in their membership, and work with matters of concern to all areas of the college. For example, in recent years as much as one-third to one-half of this provision for intensive work has been given to the effort to improve advising.

Throughout the conference period individuals are 3) *working out with the director of research* investigations in progress or to be undertaken during the succeeding year. Near the end of the conference period, sessions of the entire faculty are devoted to 4) *reports of the plans* made and work done by the smaller groups and by individuals.[52]

McCammon suggests that these experiences "offer the faculty member a solid chance to do his work better and to grow as he does it. . . . He sees from the organization of the conference that he is there to do something, not to have something done to him."[53]

Closely related to pre-college conferences are all-faculty workshops held for two or three days during the college year. The faculty at San Francisco State College has, for example, held such conferences at the conference grounds at Asilomar, some 125 miles from the college, for the purpose of studying the philosophy of general education, the needs of students, and plans for program development. In referring to one of these conferences former President J. Paul Leonard writes:

It was one of the finest educational experiences our faculty has had. . . . We worked all day, and in the evening we had square dances and games. . . . Detail jobs can be accomplished in faculty meetings once a month, but you cannot do a basic job of thinking through a philosophy with the telephone ringing and the secretary calling you or someone knocking on your door. So, we got away from it all and sat there and studied philosophy and our students.[54]

Teaching by Television. Two colleges explain that teaching by television contributes to faculty development.

At Wright Junior College, Chicago, instructors view a department chairman as he teaches over television and subsequently adopt a number of effective teaching procedures they have seen demonstrated.[55]

At Stephens College an inter-divisional course, "Ideas and Living Today," is taught over closed circuit television to all members of the entering class—divided into groups of seventeen, each with a faculty discussion leader in charge. In commenting on this plan Dean James G. Rice explains:

> The fact that at least fifty-three members of the faculty (when the lecturer is an especially stimulating one, many other faculty members sit in with the classes) have this block of common "conversational fodder" has led to a general upgrading in faculty conversation in the faculty club over coffee. . . . Meetings of discussion leaders in which the faculty leaders discuss ways of developing skill in critical thinking, more logical analysis of issues and the like has, I think, also made this project an extremely worthwhile one from the point of view of faculty development.[56]

Evaluation. A considerable number of institutions report faculty development through participation in program evaluation. Although appraisal is ordinarily carried on as a basis for considering changes and improvements in educational programs, repeated reference is made to the contributions which evaluation makes to the personal and professional growth of the staff.

Several institutions, including Michigan State University, San Francisco State College and Stephens College, report that evaluation is a continuing institution-wide process with special staff members available for coordination, leadership, and assistance to individual faculty members. These and other plans for evaluation are reported in Chapter VII and will not be repeated here except to refer to the values which such activities have for faculty improvement. Clearly the spirit of inquiry and research on educational problems fosters an atmosphere and attitude which is conducive to faculty development in the finest sense.

At Bakersfield College, the entire faculty—organized into twelve committees—took part in a survey of opportunities for, avenues to, and needs in general education at the College.[57] The major values which emerged from the survey are reported to be those which relate to faculty growth and development.[58]

Several institutions report the values which self-surveys have in stimulating faculty growth and development. At San Mateo College, for example, the entire faculty organized into nineteen committees (including those on student personnel, general education, administration, library, financial resources, public relations), worked both intensively and extensively on a self-study which is being used as a basis for institutional planning.[59]

In commenting on the study President Julio Botolazzo describes the values as follows:

1. The faculty worked as a team, and morale rose as consciousness of cooperation in a common endeavor spread.
2. Faculty members broadened their understanding of the program and problems of the College.
3. A large number of new professional friendships grew out of the experience of committee work.
4. Lines separating divisions and departments were notably softened because committee memberships cut across normal organizational patterns. It was extremely refreshing for instructors to find that virtue and wisdom were not absolutely limited to one department.[60]

In describing plans which aid faculty development at Goucher College, President Otto Kraushaar first lists "an all faculty self-evaluation extending over a period of two years. . . . The self-study was . . . chiefly an evaluation of established ends and practices, but it initiated a discussion which has been sustained."[61]

A FACULTY DEVELOPMENT PROGRAM IN ACTION

The plans described here for aiding the personal and professional growth of faculty members are representative of practices from many institutions rather than descriptions of the total programs of a few colleges. As a matter of fact, a survey of the literature of faculty improvement and an analysis of the reports and correspondence from which much of the material in this chapter is drawn reveal only one relatively comprehensive report of a college program for faculty development—McCammon's description of practices at Stephens College.[62] Perhaps the most notable characteristics of the program which McCammon describes are 1) the wide variety of activities reported, 2) the emphasis on active faculty participation, 3) the recognition given to the individual interests and concerns of staff members, and 4) the stress given to experimentation and evaluation.

No attempt will be made here to reproduce, or even summarize McCammon's accounts of what happens at Stephens College. Attention is, however, directed to the following eight types of activity which he reports effectively contribute to faculty growth:

1. *Participation in research.* With research defined as "systematic investigation of possibilities for improving administration and instruction" and with the college director of educational research available for leadership and assistance to faculty members, approximately half of the staff each year participate in one or more voluntary projects, such as experimenting with and evaluating group instruction in beginning piano classes, analyzing the use of test batteries in occupational planning, appraising the values of a science field trip, and surveying the educational achievement, employment history, community activities, and marital status of 13,000 graduates (pp. 4–7).

2. *Fall faculty conferences.* These conferences provide opportunity for faculty-wide, division, department, committee, and individual work, study and planning (pp. 7–16).

3. *Work with expert consultants.* By administrative policy, any member or group of the faculty may initiate a plan for securing a consultant to assist in meeting a problem or planning a new development. Consultants—some on single visits, others during extended periods lasting for several years—have provided expert guidance and leadership in such instructional fields as foreign languages, art, business education, and occupational planning; in college-wide programs in the improvement of reading skills, counseling and guidance; and in the evaluation of instruction (pp. 17–21).

4. *Work with national advisory boards.* Consultation with single experts has in a number of fields been extended to long-term association with committees of men and women of national distinction. These groups meet annually on campus to study and advise on college programs in their special fields of competence,

such as health education, or the use of audio-visual materials in teaching (pp. 21–31).

5. *Summer workshops.* Instructors upon occasion are employed for summer work and study on problems and develepments of concern and interest to them and the college. Under this plan instructors of the course in communication skills or coordinators of the advising programs may spend two or three weeks in evaluating past achievements and in planning for the future (pp. 32–38).

6. *Training as an adviser.* Since every faculty member serves as an adviser, a carefully planned development program (through faculty meetings, individual conferences, and through advising groups of approximately fifteen faculty members representing varied fields and interests) is provided in this area. The college emphasizes the relationship of teaching and advising and stresses that serving as an adviser has value for the personal and professional development of instructors (pp. 45–50; 66–67).

7. *Learning in the case conference.* A called conference of faculty members who work closely (teachers, advisers, and residence hall counselor, for example) with a particular student who is having marked problems is designated as a "case conference." Called to pool information about a student and her needs, and to agree upon plans for working with her, such conferences often aid participants gain new understandings, not only regarding the students under consideration but also concerning students in general (pp. 50–58).

8. *Working with librarians.* After calling attention to the fact that librarians are members of the instructional staff and are assigned to work with various departments, McCammon explains, "Librarians in common practice attend classes frequently, take active part in departmental and divisional meetings, work as members of committees, have a voice in course changes and in starting new courses. Thus the individual teacher or staff that wants information or advice from the library service need not consider an embassy on negotiations. The librarian is there beside him, on the job, every day."[63]

Additional practices which, McCammon suggests, contribute to faculty improvement include committee work, conferences with administrators, professional reading, encouraging the writing of professional books and articles, and the annual preparation of course outlines, which make recommendations for improving each course the next time it is taught.

DESIRABLE ADDITIONAL PRACTICES

Plans for faculty development which have been reported up to the present have been limited to those which are actually used. College administrators were, however, asked to report not only existing practices but also to describe additional practices which they would like to follow, or perhaps plan to follow in the future.

Several respondents wish to use plans which have been described in earlier pages of this chapter: summer workshops for curriculum planning, the release of faculty time for developing new courses or improving existing ones, the provision of funds for faculty study at, or visits to, other institutions.

The Director of Basic Studies at Western Michigan University for example suggests, "I would like to be able to offer a semester leave to an occasional staff member who is extraordinarily creative and allow him to visit other institutions, read, do research, or just think."[64]

At the College of St. Catherine, where campus workshops (in humanities in 1956 and physical sciences in 1958, for example) are an important part of the faculty development program, a desire is expressed to "enlarge program of campus workshops—subsidy needed."[65]

Former President Samuel Gould of Antioch College explains his hope for more in-term workshops: "At one time we had several . . . workshops going on . . . about once a month. Teachers visited one another's classes, talked over problems, devised new methods, etc. We hope to revive some of this kind of work next year."[66]

Repeatedly urged is a reduction in teaching load which will make more staff time available for planning and improving courses—and concomitantly result in increased faculty growth and development.

President Paul Anderson of Chatham College observes, "We wish we could afford to lighten the load of master teachers in order to provide more time for them to consult with newer faculty as to improved teaching procedures."[67]

The Chairman of the General Education Committee at Harvard University feels a need for regular staff meetings of the chairmen and young teachers in all general education courses—in addition to the present practice of having meetings of the faculty of individual courses. Pointing out that meetings of approximately two hundred staff members might be cumbersome, the suggestion is made that the staff of two or three courses might "hold a series of smaller meetings, each representing the young men in a group of courses. Such meetings might be small enough so that informal discussions might proceed successfully."[68]

From Colorado State College comes a suggestion for experimentation in teaching. "I would like to begin the practice of experimentation in general education in which various sections are organized and taught in quite different ways to see if we can find a more effective method for accomplishing the objectives of our general education program. I think the collection of evidence and the exchange of information from different experimental programs is one of the best ways to contribute to the development of a faculty."[69]

An examination of the "plans we would like to follow" proposed by administrators reveals a felt need for additional funds—to reduce teaching loads, to employ faculty members for work on curriculum development, to finance advanced study, and to finance visits to, and study at, other institutions. Recognition is appropriately given to the fact that "in-service training costs and is worth money."[70]

INEFFECTIVE PRACTICES

In corresponding with colleges a question was raised about practices found to be ineffective and which "you would, therefore, advise other colleges not to use." One college president sounds a word of warning as he writes, "I would hesitate to advise a college not to use a practice because it had not been extremely effective in our own institution."[71]

In support of this position is the fact that several colleges report as ineffective such practices as faculty study groups, faculty meetings, and staff meetings—plans which are found to be successful in other institutions.

Dean Carlin of Michigan State University speaks for a number of administrators when he asserts, "The one type of in-service training program that I would avoid and that has been unsuccessful is the program specifically labeled as an in-service training program. It has been my experience that faculty resent such programs and, therefore, resist them."[72]

A number of reports suggest that brief visits by consultants have but little value in programs of staff improvement. President Kraushaar of Goucher College, for example, finds little constructive effect in "visits by professors from other institutions who are invited to describe in a lecture or two experiments in progress . . . We have found it better to have members of our faculty visit at other institutions and spend some time observing their general education courses or programs in action, with an opportunity to discuss the aims and outcomes with both faculty and students. In this way a more thorough appraisal and evaluation is possible."[73]

Another undesirable practice reported from such divergent institutions as Harvard University and Wright Junior College is the plan of structuring and systematizing the instruction expected of young faculty members. Explains the chairman of the physical science division at Wright Junior College: "Laying out a specific program for a given instructor to follow is a practice which seems to break down rather badly. Human nature apparently is rebellious of any strait-jacketing."[74]

Echoing Kager's views are those of the Chairman of the General Education Committee at Harvard University: ". . . we have found that any attempt to systematize instruction in teaching for our younger men has not worked well. . . . In General Education, as in most Harvard education, the emphasis is on an effort to develop individuality and relatively free choice of method, both by teachers and students."[75]

CONCLUSION

Plans developed on different campuses vary as widely as the characteristics of the institutions themselves. Practices which are effective in one college may be totally unacceptable to another institution. One characteristic which appears to be common to institutions which report successful programs of faculty improvement is, however, a genuine concern by the college and its administration for individual teacher and total staff development—a concern which results in planned programs and activities involving the faculty and a concern which, within the limits of available resources, results in appropriate financial support—particularly at the point of providing faculty time for effective participation in improvement programs.

NOTES

[1] Antell, Henry, "An Inventory of Teacher Interests as a Guide Towards Their Improvement in Service." *Educational Administration and Supervision,* January 1945, p. 37.

[2] Carlin, Edward A., "How Are the Curricular, Teaching, and Personnel Problems Currently Facing Well-Established Programs of General Education Being Met?" Paper presented at Thirteenth National Conference in Higher Education, Chicago, March 3, 1958. Mimeographed, p. 3.

[3] *Report of the Second In-Service Seminar.* Carelton College, 1956. Mimeographed, pp. 5–6.

[4] *Ibid.,* p. 15.

[5] *Ibid.,* p. 15.

[6] Weintraub, Ruth G., and Deickoff, John S., "A Program of Faculty In-Service Training," *Journal of Higher Education,* October 1955, p. 346.

[7] *Ibid.,* p. 348.

[8] *Ibid.,* pp. 348–349.

[9] Letter from Richard D. Weigle, May 13, 1958.

[10] *Ibid.*

[11] Letter from Ernest Mahan, May 16, 1958.

[12] Letter from K. Ronald Bergethon, July 16, 1958.

[13] Letter from Charles C. Cole, Jr., May 2, 1958.

[14] Letter from A. L. Vaughan, April 23, 1958.

[15] Letter from Carl Kreider, May 17, 1958.
[16] Letter from Edward A. Carlin, May 5, 1958.
[17] Letter from Robert M. Limpus, May 2, 1958.
[18] Letter from Lowell E. Roberts, May 7, 1958.
[19] Letter from Dorothy H. Craven, November 15, 1958.
[20] Letter from Earl E. Edgar, June 2, 1958.
[21] Letter from Donald G. Decker, April 25, 1958.
[22] Letter from Harold Taylor, July 11, 1958.
[23] Letter from J. Paul Reynolds, July 7, 1958.
[24] Letter from Samuel B. Gould, May 7, 1958.
[25] Letter from Charles W. Cole, May 3, 1958.
[26] Letter from Sister Mary William, May 16, 1958.
[27] Letter from Herman A. Brautigam, May 5, 1958.
[28] *Ibid.*
[29] Letter from Paul R. Anderson, April 28, 1958.
[30] Letter from Robert E. Streeter, July 11, 1958.
[31] Spears, Harold, *Curriculum Planning* (New York, Prentice-Hall), 1957, p. 36.
[32] Letter from Edward A. Carlin, May 5, 1958.
[33] Letter from Joseph Axelrod, May 19, 1958.
[34] *Ibid.*
[35] Richter, Peyton E., "New Approaches to Faculty Development in a General Education Program." Typed manuscript, Boston University Junior College, 1958, p. 3.
[36] Letter from William F. Perry, May 12, 1958.
[37] Letter from Richard D. Weigle, May 13, 1958.
[38] Letter from Harold Taylor, July 11, 1958.
[39] Richter, Peyton E., *op. cit.,* pp. 4–5.
[40] Letter from Edward A. Carlin, May 5, 1958.
[41] Letter from Herman A. Brautigam, May 5, 1958.
[42] Letter from Earl E. Edgar, June 2, 1958.
[43] Letter from Kenneth B. Murdock, June 23, 1958.
[44] Letter from Herman A. Brautigam, May 5, 1958.
[45] "Teaching Workshop in General Education Courses—Summer, 1957." Antioch College, 1958. Dittoed.
[46] Report on the "Workshop in English," Orange Coast College, Costa Mesa, California, 1956. Dittoed, p. 23.
[47] Letter from Karl Kreider, May 17, 1958.
[48] *North Central Association Study on Liberal Arts Education.* Sub-Committee on Liberal Arts Education. The Commission on Research and Services of the NCA of Colleges and Secondary Schools. (No date.) Mimegraphed, p. 2.
[49] Letter from Sister M. LaBud, O.S.B., June 9, 1958.
[50] Letter from Arno Gustin, O.S.B., August 25, 1958.
[51] Letter from Carl Kreider, May 17, 1958.
[52] McCammon, Hugh, "Continuing Growth: A statement concerning the in-service training of college faculties." Stephens College, Columbia, Missouri. (No date.) Mimeographed, pp. 8–9.
[53] *Ibid.,* p. 9.
[54] Leonard, J. Paul, "Building a Curriculum for Student Needs at San Francisco State College," in Stickler, W. Hugh, editor, *Organization and Administration of General Education* (Dubuque, Wm. C. Brown Co.), 1951, p. 189.

[55] Letter from Sumner Scott, July 3, 1958.
[56] Letter from James G. Rice, May 19, 1958.
[57] *Opportunities in General Education*. Bakersfield College, Bakersfield, California, 1951. Mimeographed.
[58] Letter from Thomas B. Merson, June 2, 1958.
[59] *Summary Reports of the Faculty Self-Study Committees*. College of San Mateo, San Mateo, California, 1957. Mimeographed.
[60] Letter from Julio L. Bortolazzo, Nov. 25, 1958.
[61] Letter from Otto F. Kraushaar, August 12, 1958.
[62] McCammon, Hugh, *op. cit.*
[63] *Ibid.*, p. 71.
[64] Letter from Robert M. Limpus, May 2, 1958.
[65] Letter from Sister Mary William, May 16, 1958.
[66] Letter from Samuel B. Gould, May 7, 1958.
[67] Letter from Paul R. Anderson, April 28, 1958.
[68] Letter from Kenneth B. Murdock, June 23, 1958.
[69] Letter from Donald G. Decker, April 25, 1958.
[70] McCammon, Hugh, *op. cit.*, p. 96.
[71] Letter from Donald G. Decker, April 25, 1958.
[72] Letter from Edward A. Carlin, May 5, 1958.
[73] Letter from Otto F. Kraushaar, August 12, 1958.
[74] Letter from P. Kager, May 16, 1958.
[75] Letter from Kenneth B. Murdock, June 23, 1958.

Chapter VII

METHODS OF EVALUATION AND RESEARCH

PAUL L. DRESSEL
Director of Institutional Research,
Michigan State University

THE invention and perfection of academic arithmetic provides higher education with evaluation devices of previously unparalleled and devastating objectivity. The admission of a student is predicated on 15 high school units; his college progress is measured in credits and points; his graduation is assured by his acquiring 120 properly distributed semester hours. The success of commencement is gauged by the number of honorary degrees awarded. Departments are staffed, budgeted, and even rated by the number of courses and hours offered. Universities are distinguished from colleges by the number of deans, and the success of either is measured by the number of graduates listed in *Who's Who*. Such crude quantitative appraisal is so extensively used and so seriously regarded as to have far reaching results.

The acceptance of course credits as the units of achievement, accompanied by the tradition—sometimes mistakenly regarded as an aspect of academic freedom—that the instructor is the sole judge of grade and hence of credit, fosters continuing resistance to any effort to evaluate instruction. Likewise, evaluation of student progress over periods of time inclusive of several courses becomes well nigh meaningless. Instructors can readily ignore the results as inapplicable to their particular course. Students, who see grades and credits as the currency of the academic realm, argue that that currency cannot be declared counterfeit after having been accepted and credited to their account. Evaluation—which might actually provide an analysis and basis for the improvement of the educational process—is unwelcome because it threatens or complicates this straightforward arithmetical procedure, which preserves for the instructor and department the utmost autonomy and assigns to the registrar the custody of simple records which are readily maintained and easily summarized into largely irrelevant statistical reports.

When practices are stated thus baldly, disclaimers arise on all sides, but the fact remains that few colleges in these United States arise above this bookkeeping caricature of measuring educational achievement. Much of the concern for revivification of liberal education arises out of this credit accumulation conception of a degree. If 120 semester hours is to be equated to a degree, who is to say that this course or these three credits is more appropriate than that—particularly when every course and every department is staffed with enthusiastic proponents of the virtues of that particular discipline? Departments and courses therein arise out of arbitrary, and often quite artificial, subdivisions of knowledge—yet these subdivisions become increasingly important, to the point where trespass is grounds for accusation of unprofessional conduct. Unfortunately, the objectives of liberal education embrace ideas, values, and methods of inquiry not accommodated to these subdivisions, and so they are relegated to the early pages of the college bulletin. There they cause no trouble, for the knowing reader leaves them unread as he immediately turns to the listing of courses and requirements which constitute the operational definition of the institution's conception of an education.

Any real improvement in education must come through methods of evaluation which afford what the present parody of evaluation by credit accumulation does not afford—evidence on the relevance and efficacy of educational experience in producing desired changes in students. The remainder of this chapter is devoted to consideration of conceptions of evaluation which might thus improve education. Whether that improved education is called general, liberal, or something else is largely irrelevant. The desired characteristics cannot be evoked by providing a new label.

THE ROLE OF EVALUATION IN CURRICULUM DEVELOPMENT

Selecting and Clarifying Objectives. The evaluation of any educational program must be with reference to the purposes of the program. Though stated or explicit objectives are usually available, these should not too readily be accepted as the actual purposes, for they are often general, ethereal, and quite unrelated to the day-to-day teaching-learning process. The objectives implicit in a course circumscribed by the use of a particular textbook are very real and very clear to the students, but these objectives may be largely irrelevant to the explicit ultimate goals stated in the bulletin. Only if the immediate implicit objectives of each course have direct relevance to the explicit ultimate objectives will these latter objectives be functional.

Objectives may and reasonably should vary from college to college and the same objective may have even different implications, depending upon the locale and the clientele. Accordingly each institution should define with some care the characteristics of the students it will admit, or alternatively, study carefully the characteristics of those that it does admit. Without suggesting that the needs of students completely dictate the educational program to be provided, it is clear that the needs of students in a small Negro college in Mississippi are not entirely identical with those of students admitted to Harvard.

Colleges are instruments of society. As such they are subject to social pressures. The technological and scientific bent of present-day society has had obvious impact on the college of today when it is contrasted with that of one hundred years ago. Demands for courses in Russian and Arabic exemplify the force of these pressures; classical education with its emphasis on the past has given place to a more utilitarian conception. College faculties must consider from time to time the needs of society and reconsider objectives in terms of their interpretation of these needs. The failure to do so only results in gradual, even unconscious, acquiescence to continuing pressure.

Professional organizations, and scholars in particular disciplines, from time to time suggest different emphases and purposes, and develop new syntheses of subject matter. For example, the nature and purposes of introductory courses in mathematics and physics are presently under re-examination.

From such sources, many objectives can be collected or deduced. The too ready solution of dealing with this superabundance of objectives by subdivision and assignment of objectives to particular courses and departments should be avoided. It is only another route to compartmentalization and to premature overspecialization. Some procedure must be found to reduce objectives to a manageable number of significant ones with transcendent implications which restore to higher education a unity of purpose largely lost through the emphasis on courses and credits. If a faculty can agree on some broad philosophical principles which describe at once the kind of person and the kind of world they deem desirable, some purposes will become more important than others. Indeed, the entire curriculum may develop out of such agreement. St. John's College at Annapolis is a notable example.

Recourse to what is known about the nature of motivation and the learning process provides another basis for selection among objectives. A course in philosophy based on the concerns of mature individuals in the later years of life is unlikely to hold much appeal to youth of college age. The assimilation of information and skills proceeds but haltingly when the tasks lack perspective and purpose and when they either are or appear to be unrelated to interests and goals of the learner. The objectives of the good teacher derive from knowledge of his students as well as from knowledge of his subject.

Selecting and Planning Relevant Experiences. Formal education provides a set of experiences planned with the expectation that certain results will ensue in individuals having these experiences. The range of educational experiences available is as limitless as that of the composite experience of mankind, although considerations of economy, prudence, and relevancy quickly impose some restrictions. These restrictions are less rigorous than the barrenness of many classrooms would suggest. Textual materials, laboratories, reading lists, library browsing, and a wide range of audio-visual materials are readily available for most classes. Teaching methods, varying from authoritarian formal lectures to ultra-democratic and sometimes chaotic leaderless groups, may be selected and adapted to the course purposes and to teacher and student personality. Work experience, field trips, and foreign study are additional types of experiences used by some colleges. Most campuses offer or could offer many cultural experiences in addition to the traditional classroom. The selection among these many possible experiences and the planning of additional ones on the basis of their obvious relevance to the avowed objectives are necessary for effective education.

Such choice and planning demand evaluation to determine whether the apparent relevancy of experience to goals is justified by the effect on students. Student awareness of the goals and of the relation between goals and experience may be a necessary pre-condition for effectiveness. Evaluation contributes to this awareness.

The Organization of Educational Experience. The effect of the course-credit system is most apparent in the lack of organization for integration in the curriculum and the consequent lack of impact on students. The truly significant outcomes of education are not accomplished through single courses nor in short periods of time. Those integrative concepts, principles, and methods of inquiry which represent the major outcomes of education must be held continuously before students, and the treatment of them must be ever deeper and more inclusive levels of understanding. Such integrative ideas also make evident the relations between disciplines and between formal learning and problems of individuals and society. The planning of an integrated and integrative educational experience is complicated by the rich array of course offerings which minimize the common experiences of students. Courses which should be sequential or supplementary either become overlapping and repetitive or are so delimited as to avoid this, because there is no assurance that all students have had the related courses. The proper sequence of experiences for the promotion of integrative learning is uncertain and the integrative capacities of individuals at various educational levels are largely unknown. These problems are complex and only through careful and extended study are better answers than those now accepted to be found. At the moment, the problems are largely ignored.

Evaluation. Evaluation—in the form of studies of student characteristics, surveys of social demands, comparisons of the effectiveness of various materials and methods, and the organizations thereof—has been noted as a necessary phase of the first stages in the planning of a curriculum. Even so, the complex composite will involve many judgments, the validity of which can only be determined by study of the total impact of the curriculum in moving individuals in the directions specified by objectives. Such broad and long term evaluation may point to weaknesses or imbalances which require restudy. In the process of planning and evaluation, alternative programs will occur which hold promise of enhanced achievement. Changes in the nature of the students or of the faculty may destroy the effectiveness of once excellent practices. Curricula must be recurringly examined, and evaluation is the means for so doing.

APPROACHES TO EVALUATION

Two distinct and supplementary approaches to evaluation have been mentioned. The first of these is the study of the educational process; the second is the study of the results. If a course does not offer experiences directly related to objectives, the amount of change in students in reference to these objectives will be less than it could be, and whatever change is found cannot logically be credited to the course.

If, for example, a science teacher states that as one result of this course students should display a continuing interest in science, and if the reading and discussion with others of articles or current science developments is viewed as a manifestation of this objective, the experience of the course should be relevant to this purpose. If this teacher depends on a typical chemistry text and laboratory "cookbook" to the exclusion of any other activity which would be likely to contribute to the stated objective, such interest as individual students might develop would most likely be evidenced by their taking more chemistry. The teacher might make available periodicals and books containing such reports on science and encourage students to read and report on them for extra credit. He might plan to relate the course materials to current articles at every opportunity. An even more intensive experience would result if all students were provided with copies of certain periodicals and required to read certain articles, to prepare for a class discussion each week. A composite of all these and other approaches would highlight the objective even more. It might also overemphasize it to the detriment of other important objectives.

These various patterns of experience imply different views of the nature of learning, or of the function of education. The teacher who emphasizes chemistry may feel that reading current science articles is really not an appropriate or desirable outcome of his course or—arguing from an earlier and discredited conception of the transfer of training—he may be convinced that all other objectives flow out of the discipline of the mind through mastery of subject matter. The encouragement of reading as a supplemental activity implies the provision of an opportunity without interfering with the main purpose of the course. Reference (by teachers) to current articles and developments recognizes that motivation and interest are aroused by a demonstration of the relevance of the material, and that the values, practices, and views of the teacher may affect those of the student. The placing of current articles in the hands of students with the requirement that they read and discuss them recognizes that such direct contact with the materials and the recurrent experience of reading them may develop a habit which will continue after completion of the course. This approach also recognizes that the student may have to develop some skills in reading science articles and that the development of these is as important as any other activity which might be assigned class time.

There is little point in attempting to measure student development with regard to objectives largely ignored in teaching. On the other hand, learning is so complex a process and objectives are so inter-related that one cannot assume that the experiences selected are having the effects anticipated. If the science teacher is concerned with a *continuing* interest in science evidenced by reading and discussion of scientific articles, then the evidence of success is to be sought not during, nor at the close of, but after completion of the course, perhaps even after completion of college. Through the seeking of such evidence the potency of the experiences provided by the textbook-oriented chemistry teacher may be compared with those provided in other courses giving more attention to science articles. But the results may be misleading, for a course may fail of its purpose because of the teacher's personality, or an antagonism to science experienced by the students in concurrent or following religion or humanities courses.

Both study of the process and of the immediate and ultimate results are necessary in understanding and improving the educational process.

Study of the Process. The relevancy of the educational process to purposes can be studied by considering whether the experiences require the behavior implied by those purposes. The way in which a student perceives the experience and the feelings he has about them require study since these may determine the effect of the experience. Accordingly it is appropriate to seek answers to such questions as:

1. What does the student perceive as the real objectives of a course or college?
2. What values does he attach to taking each course and why?
3. What does he think about the quality of instruction provided?

4. How does he study for various courses, what does he regard as the important things to do to acquire a satisfactory grade?

5. What is the impact on the student of various materials and teaching techniques?

6. To what extent does each student engage himself with ideas and issues in contrast to waiting for someone to provide the appropriate answer for recording in the ubiquitous notebook?

7. To what extent do students regard particular pairs of courses as independent, repetitious, supplemental, or sequential?

With slight rewording, these and other questions may be posed for answering by the course instructor and by other members of the faculty.

As worded, these questions suggest only an opinion-polling type of evaluation. However, as Bloom and Broder[1] have shown in their study of the effect of instruction on students, reasonably clear snapshots can be taken of the mental activity of students in the classroom by use of stimulated recall techniques. Essays, discussions, observation, critical incidents, recording and analysis of entire class periods, check lists, rating scales, anecdotal records, records of library usage, are some of the many ways in which insight into the effect of the educational process on an individual may be gained. Those interested in group behavior may wish to analyze the various types of interaction going on, including the leader and follower roles of individuals. From such study, certain principles gradually emerge. For example, until students begin interacting with each other rather than seeking to make statements which will receive approval by the instructor, little real progress in case study techniques is likely to take place.

There are a number of values which arise out of evaluation which concentrates on study of the educational process. All too little is known about the nature of learning and this little is often unknown to college teachers. The habit of awareness and concern about the effect on the student of any classroom activity needs to be cultivated. Out of this soon arises an awareness that not all individuals react in the same manner, not necessarily because of inability or perverseness, but because each person's perception of a new experience is colored by what he is through heredity and past experience. Misunderstanding or lack of understanding on the part of a student may indicate a failure in instruction—not just, as is commonly assumed, a failure on the part of the student. One value, then, of process study is that the instructor becomes increasingly sensitive to differences in students and to the effect of various teaching and learning experiences in relation to these differences.

A second value arises out of the student's realization that his understanding and his ideas are of real importance to the teacher. This being true, most students will become increasingly concerned about their educational development rather than resting content with learning which emphasizes giving back to the instructor what that instructor emphasizes. Students in the course and credit milieu are terribly grade conscious. Since a degree is equated to the acquiring of courses and credits, it appears to them to be unfair to make the grade in one course obviously dependent upon achievement in preceding ones. This is even carried to the extreme of questioning the instructor as to whether successive tests in a single course will cover material included in previous tests. By making it apparent to the student that his understanding and his organization of knowledge are at least as important as the coverage of content, a different view may gradually be cultivated.

At this point a third possible value—*gradual* acceptance by the student of responsibility for his own education—must be recognized and sought, else the previous two will be lost. Here perhaps an example will make the point. At Michigan State University, special honors sections were organized to provide more challenge for the able student. Some instructors viewed these only as opportunities to cover more material. Others assumed that these students of high ability would be largely self-directed. Either tactic met with resistance on the part of students and disappointment on the part of the instructor. Getting students to take responsibiliy for their own education requires a change in the students—especially when, as was clearly the case with these students, their past educational experience and their concurrent experiences structured their expectations to conform with instructor requirements. Developing the student's interest, initiative, and responsibility in educating himself is a worthy objective and one which must be gradually developed through experiences which provide for increasing personal responsibility and self-evaluation.

As one becomes concerned with the cumulative impact of sequentially planned experiences, study of the process merges with study of the results. Knowledge which is unorganized and unrelated is soon forgotten. Intellectual abilities which are not actually required and used in increasingly complex tasks are not developed. Feelings and attitudes which are unrecognized may impede learning. Desirable habits and skills require repetition until they become fixed. Study of the effectiveness of the cumulative impact of education is, in actuality, a study of the results achieved up to that moment.

Study of the Results. Although the educational process and the results of that process are inter-related and at times indistinguishable, the final evaluation of any educational program must be in terms of its results. The evaluation need not be limited to those results which are avowed purposes of the program, for there may be unexpected and even untoward results of an educational program. However, it is not justifiable to claim for a program the development of all of the desirable characteristics found in the graduates.

Every teacher engages in some evaluation of the effectiveness of his teaching. Even the apparent failure to do so in itself evidences a kind of evaluation, and not necessarily a favorable one. In engaging in such informal, unsystematic evaluation, the teacher is prone to reflect upon the individual case: the almost miraculous change in point of view, continuation into graduate study in the field, or the gratifying tribute to the values of that particular course. Such judgments equate effectiveness of teaching with the creation, out of students, of persons in the teacher's image.

Institutions evaluating their programs are likewise given to looking at the success of graduates in professional or graduate schools, at income level, at the names of graduates found in *Who's*

Who, and at a variety of other factors which may be irrelevant to the stated objectives of the institution. A more insightful kind of evaluation is difficult. The real purposes of education are to be found in changes which augment the inner resources of the individual, but it is no less difficult with graduates than with undergraduates to find out what kind of people they really are and what sort of inner resources they have. Moreover, the range of experiences which individuals have had in the years after graduation from college make it impossible to sort out those qualities molded out of the college experience and those primarily the result of other experiences. By reducing the number of years out of college to, say five, the range of experiences following college graduation is automatically reduced. However, other factors are involved which may interfere with a determination of the significance of college experience. The years immediately after college are ones in which the graduates are adjusting to a job, raising a family, buying a home, and in other ways engaging in activities which interfere with achieving a stable position in a community, or with participation in cultural or service activities which they may greatly desire and enjoy.[2]

Attractive as it is, the idea of evaluating the effectiveness of college education by a study of the graduates some years afterward is not feasible. The evaluation of the kinds of changes to which colleges are committed cannot be accomplished solely by paper and pencil means. The expense of observation and interviewing techniques and the amount of time required of the student and evaluator alike make systematic follow-ups of graduates impossible except in isolated cases wherein special funds become available. *Such evaluation as is done must be done largely within the span of time that the student remains in school.* This is as it should be, for if the period in which the student is in college produces no determinable changes, then it would seem unreasonable to argue that any characteristics emergent at some later date are results of the college experience. The purposes of college are not to determine what an individual will be like several years after college but to provide him with resources out of which he can improve himself. If these resources are clearly defined, and if they have been developed, they should be detectable. Accordingly, colleges will do well to focus on the study of results at the end of one, two, three, and four years of college at a point where the evidence has some immediate implication with regard to curriculum organization and teaching practices.

This matter of the utility of the results of evaluation is another reason for refusing to defer study of results to the graduates. Evidence on graduates after they are out of college fifteen to twenty years has little meaning to the current faculty in an institution. In the first place, the nature of the program at the time these graduates were in school is no longer known in sufficient detail to have any implications for curriculum planning. In the second place, the existing curriculum and faculty at the time the evaluation is done are so different in nature from those of the earlier period that the faculty has no concern about the results. This is even a problem on shorter periods; it is not unusual to find, in an institution in which courses are under continual reorganization, that by the time an evaluation study is completed on a course, sufficient change will have been made that the faculty consider the evaluation evidence worthless. Evaluation that is very far removed from the time of instruction falls on barren ground.

Perhaps the major point in all of this is that too many individuals see evaluation as something that comes after the planning of a curriculum rather than as a vital part of that planning. From the conversation of faculty members, one gets the impression that much in the way of "experimentation" is being done in our education. In actuality, someone does something a little differently without collecting evidence to judge whether the new venture is superior to that which it replaced. *Any evaluation activity which is to be long maintained as a significant part of a program must be closely related to accepted educational goals, must have implications for the improvement of curriculum, and must lead to decisions and actions of sufficient importance to cause everyone concerned to feel that the effort spent in evaluation is well repaid.*

SPECIFIC EVALUATION PRACTICES

Course Examinations and Grading. Course examinations and grades force students to work, but they also circumscribe learning. The explicit objectives of a course are often contravened by the objectives implicit in the course of examinations and in the grades based upon these. There are some desirable educational outcomes upon which an individual should not be graded. One might, for example, hope that an individual taking his first course in an area would develop some interest in and appreciation for that area. It is conceivable, however, that he might end up with an "A" in the course even though he disliked the course and everything that it represented very bitterly. This dislike should not enter into the final grade. Any grading policy which permits this to happen will foster insincerity and dishonesty on the part of the student. If such dislike is prevalent, however, the teacher should consider whether the nature of the course, the examinations, and the grading may explain the dislike of the course. Evidence of the students' reactions to the course is relevant to the improvement of the course but not to the grading of it.

Those objectives which are not going to be a part of the grade should be stated and the policy frankly explained to the student. These "ungraded" objectives include some of the most important objectives of education. Specifically they include all those dealing with attitudes and values. Motivating students to work for something not incorporated in their grade is part of the task of teaching. Examinations and grades need not control entirely the efforts of students, and whether they do or not depends very largely on the point of view cultivated by the teachers. If evidence is sought so that both student and instructor can determine the success of the course in respect to these "ungraded" objectives, adequate motivation will be provided for most students.

Examinations for grading should also take on a tone of realism not now commonly present. For example, one of the best bits of evidence as to the achievement of a student in a particular course is his ability to read, understand, and utilize new materials not studied in the classroom, even materials which may be slightly more difficult than those treated in the particular course. The use of tasks which require extended thought on the part of students, and the possibility of associating such tasks with an open-book type of examination suggest problems in time involvement. Concern about security, honesty, and the fifty-minute class schedule are only part of this problem. There is a point of view that learning is suspended during an examination period. This results naturally from the fact that hours and credits are assigned on the basis of what the teacher does rather than what the student does. Nevertheless, a truly significant examination is a real learning experience and might well be extended over several periods rather than one.

Another dubious examination practice is that of assigning a grade on every examination. Ideally, an appraisal coming at the end of a course should be the basis for deciding what the student has accomplished. A student who does poorly in work early in the quarter but is able to handle everything at an "A" level at the end deserves an "A." Likewise a student performing at an "A" level during most of the quarter but failing a final examination deserves a failure, barring illness or some other mitigating factor. However, the view that basing a grade on performance at the end of the course is more satisfactory than averaging grades over the course, assumes a cumulative quality to the course and to the examination which is not always present. Nevertheless, the use of an examination or other evaluation device to help the student re-examine and improve his own work is reduced by assignment of a grade. A grade has an element of finality and signifies completion of a task. The student who receives a "C" on a theme has no incentive to rewrite it, whereas an indication of the inadequacies accompanied by suggestions for rewriting might provide some real motivation for improvement. So long as we insist on treating a course and each segment thereof as a unit and assigning a grade to it, attention of students will be focused on some of the most easily tested, but often least significant, aspects of a course.

Selection and Placement. The selection and placement of students in college are part of the so-called problem of articulation between the secondary school and college. This problem is always a current one, but its nature shifts with changing social conditions. At one time the high school was regarded as largely college preparatory in nature, but gradually the emphasis changed with the secondary school, more responsible to the vast majority not going on to college. Now once again, as the percentage of youth going to college rises, preparation for college is being viewed as a major obligation of the secondary school.

Colleges, too, may have to reconsider their point of view about selection and placement of students. In the face of evidence accumulated a few years ago that specific subjects in high school had no great relevance to success in college, many colleges have shifted to selection primarily in terms of high school grades and scores on aptitude tests rather than evidence of achievement relative to major fields of knowledge and the objectives of higher education. While it is true that the lack of specific courses in science or mathematics or language in the high school does not necessarily mark a student for failure in college, it is clear that his selection of fields is delimited and that for many curricula additional time must be required in order to complete a college degree. Both high schools and colleges have tried to ignore this, and the latter have even compensated for it by giving high school courses for college credit. If once again college-going students are required to take chemistry, physics, mathematics, and foreign language in high school, the blithe assumption made by many college faculty members that high school courses make no difference must be re-examined. The motivation of a freshman is quickly dampened by repetition. The Advanced Placement Program of the College Entrance Examination Board, although it emphasizes primarily standard departmental college courses offered to gifted high school seniors, represents a step in this direction.

In the general education area, where the achievement of the student is less likely to be determined entirely by the courses which he has taken, the problem of assessment of the student's status with regard to general education objectives is a pressing one. More of our selection, orientation, and placement activity should be based upon achievement type of examinations which measure the competencies of students relative to the broad areas of knowledge and general education type objectives. In contrast with looking at high school grades and credits and evidence of aptitude for college work, the achievement type testing program would permit an institution to place a student in courses and at a level suitable to his achievement. In some cases this might mean saying forthrightly to the student that if he pursues a certain objective, it will require as much as five years rather than the usual four to acquire a degree. For another student it might mean placement at an advanced level in certain fields with the possibility that college credit for the earlier work would be permitted.

Such decisions will not be made unless the testing program includes the material and the objectives about which the faculty is concerned and in regard to which they hope to see progress. Such a testing program would provide a base for comparison with comprehensive examinations given at the end of the sophomore or senior year. Tests of guidance type involving aptitudes, interests, and personality are not irrelevant to college planning, but the results are to a large extent irrelevant to the concerns of faculty members teaching particular courses. Furthermore, the impact of a freshman testing program based largely upon "aptitudes" is to give the student the false impression of the major purposes of the institution. The tendency in selection and guidance testing is to develop tests on the basis of correlation with grades and even to select tests which are devoid of specific content. Such tests, therefore, have no direct implications either for the quality or lack thereof in the preceding secondary school instruction, nor for the planning of college level instruction. If a college program is based upon certain assumptions about the previous preparation of the students, the tests given at the time of selection or admission should provide the basis for determining whether students admitted meet these assumptions.

Evaluation of Courses and Curricula. Any new development in education is greeted by demands for evaluation of it. This implication that existing educational practices have been evaluated and found to be good is clearly unjustified. Hallowed educational practice is not necessarily good, and it certainly is not always the most effective means of education. New or experimental practices have no greater need for evaluation than existing ones, but they should take shape in part on the basis of accumulation of evidence. The disinclination of individuals involved in formulating a new program to engage in evaluation until the program has become set, is unjustified.

All too much of the attention to evaluation takes place at the level of individual courses. This continues to be true in the context of concern about general education, for even though the problem of general education arises out of specialization and departmentalization, faculty members seldom proceed far in the development of a program of general education before breaking the program down into specific courses. These then are assigned to relatively specialized faculty members who make of each course a new specialty. Naturally, then, evaluation tends to take place at the course level. Here there arise two major alternatives. First of all, the general education course may be seen as supplanting one or more introductory departmental courses and the attempt may be undertaken to compare the effectiveness of these two. Usually this is wasted effort. The traditional departmental course, if it is what the description implies, emphasizes content materials selected for the individual continuing in the field. When objectives differ there is no basis for comparing the effectiveness of the two courses. So, too, an evaluation of the adequacy of a general education course as a substitute for the first departmental course is commonly impossible because the student must still take the first departmental course if he wishes to continue in the field. One reason for the demand for comparison of traditional and new courses is that the general education course differs but little from the traditional course other than in selection of content. Saying that an objective of a course is critical thinking does not make it so unless the whole plan of instruction in the course is examined carefully in terms of its relationship to this objective. This emphasizes the need for the second type of evaluation in which alternative formulations of a course are compared as to their effectiveness in producing changes in regard to specified objectives.

More studies of the type carried out at Wright Junior College by Hymen Chausow are needed. This study involved variations of general education social science courses in terms of their contribution to the objective of critical thinking. The existing pattern of instruction was maintained in some sections; in other sections somewhat greater emphasis was placed upon critical thinking, using the same outline and the same materials as in the first type of course. A third variation was introduced in which any attempt to cover all of the customary materials was abandoned in favor of careful planning of the day-by-day activity in reference to this major objective of critical thinking. Unusual in this study was the fact that the nature of the classroom experience was planned in some detail and there were real differences existing between the three levels of instruction with respect to the objective. The results corresponded with the hypothesis. That is to say, the sections planned definitely in terms of the objective showed far greater gains in critical thinking than did the others. Despite acceptance of the objective of critical thinking, the previously existing pattern of instruction was demonstrated to make very little contribution to the objective.

In respect to such an objective, however, the amount of change to be expected as a result of any single course cannot be very large. Furthermore, there is doubt that even if some gain is found in connection with a single course, that this gain will have very much significance with respect to the student's behavior in other areas of activity. From the general education point of view, what is needed is that certain pervasive objectives be made the prime attention of a whole group of courses. Evaluation at the level of the total curriculum rather than evaluation at the level of single courses is the crying need.

Comprehensive Examinations. This need for evaluation over

a period of time, over more than one course, and over more than one discipline suggests the importance of comprehensive examinations. Such examinations, as well as having the qualities already suggested, should involve objectives which are significant in many courses, and they should be so designed as to require the student to organize and utilize information and abilities from all of his prior experience rather than the factual recall of specific information already taught and tested for in single courses. Some of the values of comprehensive examinations are found in the following:

1. They enforce a review and integration of previous work. This is true both for the students taking the examination and for the faculty who are required to prepare it.
2. The examination focuses the attention of students and faculty on the broad goals of education which transcend the individual courses or departments.
3. Emphasis is placed on the educational development of the student rather than on his accumulation of courses and credits.
4. A comprehensive examination profile provides evidence on strengths and weaknesses as a basis for planning the next stage of the educational program.
5. Since the end of the first two years of college is becoming increasingly a critical point with regard to higher education, a comprehensive examination at that point can be a basis for screening of those permitted to continue toward a degree. Likewise, a senior comprehensive may be a major factor in determining whether a student should receive a degree. Such decisions reinforce the idea that there is more to acquiring a college education than the accumulataion of courses, credits, and honor points.
6. A basis is provided for re-examination of the requirements of the course content and the instructional methods. If the single student performs badly in an area, this may be considered the student's fault. But if an entire group of students does poorly on some aspect of an examination, the curriculum and instruction may need overhauling.
7. Comprehensive examinations can become a basis for granting credit to students without formal enrollment in class. This provides a ready means of acceleration. If the principle of acceleration is not accepted, the examination still provides a basis for better placement of the student.

Despite all of the attention to comprehensive examinations in American higher education, they have been notably successful in only a few colleges. This is because, as already noted, they compete with courses and credits as the major means of evaluating progress. The examination becomes only an additional hurdle to the student and a source of extra work for the faculty. The development, analysis, interpretation, and use of the results of a good comprehensive examination is an arduous task. Commercially available tests, such as the Graduate Record examinations or the Sequential Tests of Educational Progress, may be useful provided that the faculty studies these in detail in advance of using them and accepts the examinations as having applicability to their program. However, these examinations, because of their essentially objective character and wide applicability, cannot cover all the outcomes desired. The ability to organize knowledge, creativity or originality in thinking, and increased insight into values are challenging evaluation tasks. Only the teacher who has attempted them will fully realize the difficulty of teaching for such objectives, and this value is largely lost if the comprehensive examination is restricted to the use of commercial tests and programs.

Comprehensive examinations as used at Antioch College apparently have become an accepted part of the program. Requirements are waived, credits are granted, and extra work may be required as a result of the examinations. The integrative demands of the examination are accepted alike by students and faculty. Likewise, at the General College of the University of Minnesota the comprehensive examination plays a major role. One form is given as a pre-test to aid in planning the student's program. It is repeated at the end of the freshman year to assess progress and to help plan his sophomore year. Finally, the examination is given again at the end of the sophomore year to reach a decision as to whether he has satisfactorily completed the two-year program.

Comprehensive examinations may—and indeed should—involve written and oral procedures. One interesting practice in combining these procedures requires the student to first take a written examination. This is carefully read by a number of faculty members from various fields who then develop a set of questions for the oral examination. Such a comprehensive places a premium not only on knowing and organizing the knowledge of several fields, but also upon both written and oral expression. Thus it is a truly integrative experience.

Evaluation of Instruction. The nature of doctoral training has tended to focus the attention of college teachers on the knowledge of content materials and on the organization of knowledge which have been of particular interest to specialists in the various fields. The ways of the neophyte are not, however, always the same as those of the scholar. Scholar and teacher are not equivalent terms.

The disinclination to use the term teacher at the college level in favor of the term instructor or professor has usually been taken as an indication that teacher was regarded as an inferior designation. On the other hand, it may be that many college professors have subconsciously recognized that they were not really teaching. One may lecture on much the same level as tossing feed to chickens. Teaching involves somewhat more responsibility to students. First, the teacher accepts some responsibility for the motivation of the student by helping him to understand the significance of what is to be learned. This motivation can be accomplished in part by making clear the basic purposes and objectives of the course. It can be accomplished in part by showing some of the uses of knowledge, abilities, and skills learned in the course. In part it can be accomplished by relating materials dealt with in the course and experiences which students have had, may be having, or are likely to have outside of the course. In part, also, motivation can be supplied by demonstrating a real interest in the individual student and in his reactions to any problems in dealing with the course.

Higher education in the present day has been sold largely on the basis of the economic significance. Indeed at the moment many individuals are arguing that the student ought to be made in one way or another to pay for the total expenses of his college education on the grounds that it eventually enhances his income by many thousands of dollars. The teacher who does not accept this point of view may be irritated by finding it in his students, but he should keep in mind that this motivation is not entirely the student's fault. Developing better motivation is heavily a responsibility of the teacher.

The second and closely related function of the teacher is to encourage and reward the students and thereby to provide some satisfaction to the students. All too much of our testing and our reading of papers emphasizes faults and errors without equally pointing to some of the good qualities and providing suggestions for other improvements thereby giving the student some satisfaction as well as some incentive for other efforts. The time requirement for this kind of encouragement may become quite heavy, but it is largely this kind of individual attention which justifies low teacher-student ratios.

A third way in which the teacher can contribute to a student's learning is through assisting him to react in an appropriate manner. When a youngster is learning how to hold and use a baseball bat he may be guided through the swinging of the bat a number of times. This experience is more effective than demonstration, for it involves action rather than observation. Complex acts, whether physical or mental, are composed of too many elements for an observer to grasp readily. For example, college assignments requiring the reading of science and mathematical material are not taken seriously by many students or even by the teachers. The teacher knows by experience that most of the students cannot and will not read and understand the material and the students know from past experience that the teacher will explain it. If the ability to read such material for oneself is as important as many teachers believe it to be, then the students should be guided through the reading and interpreting of such materials until they acquire some facility.

Another way in which the teacher helps the student to learn is by planning the sequence of classroom experiences carefully so that a continuity in ideas, principles, and procedures is apparent to the student. If what the student learns today can be perceived by him in relationship to what has been learned yesterday and what he is going to study tomorrow, his total learning experience will take on greater meaning and become something other than the matter of learning isolated bits of information day by day. If this ordering of experience can also involve interrelationships with other fields and other courses—even other experiences of the student outside of the classroom—the total significance of the learning will be increased with the resulting higher level of motivation on the part of the student.

The viewing of teaching in this manner leads to a somewhat different approach to the evaluation of instruction than has often been used. Collection of student reactions to the instructor and the class has often placed too much emphasis on teacher characteristics in their effect on changes in students. A more effective evaluation is achieved by directing attention to the learning process. In so doing the student is asked to become self-analytical, to study his own role in, and perception of, the class rather than to engage himself with a judgment of the teacher's conduct of the class. Accordingly, it would seem to be appropriate to ask students what they perceive to be the goals of a particular course. If the goals perceived by the students coincide with those in the mind of the instructor, it would appear that students and teachers are working to the same ends. The students might next be asked what they perceive to be the relationship between the course experiences which are provided and the goals which they see in the course. Here recurring experiences in interviewing students with regard to general education courses suggest that the student often perceives no relationship between what he is asked to do day by day and the stated purposes of the course. When this is true, one of two things is happening. Either the instructor fails to interpret to students the relationship of instruction with the purposes of the course or the experiences are not closely related to the stated objectives. In either case some action is suggested.

The student may also be asked to indicate his habits of study. If he perceives certain goals which he is expected to attain in the course, it may be anticipated that he has developed some methods of achieving those goals. His habits of study may be revealing of what the goals really mean to him and may point also to some further need on the part of the instructor in clarifying what is expected of the student in the way of preparation. Again the student might be asked what tangible effects the course has had on him. While it is not to be expected that any particular course will have marked effect on every student, every course should somewhat influence the views of many of the students and it should result in some alteration of the plans of a few. If students report no such effects, or if the effects reported are unanticipated, some further consideration is dictated. Finally, it appears appropriate to ask the students for specific suggestions for improvement not only in what the instructor does but also of the entire learning process.

Such an approach as this tends to focus the student's attention on the basic purposes of the course, on the relationship between those purposes and the experiences provided, and on his own behavior and preparation with regard to the course. The replies collected should be useful to the instructor in careful examination of his instructional practices and of course materials. Continuing use of this approach to evaluation should develop a great self-consciousness and concern, on the part of the students, for the accumulative significance of their educational experience.

There are, of course, many other ways to evaluate instruction. Interclass visitation by instructors, recordings of classroom activity, analysis of examination content, of the behavior required to answer examination questions, and to complete the day-to-day assignments—all point to ways in which the instructional process can be viewed more carefully in terms of the avowed purposes. Changes induced in the students provide the ultimate check on the quality of the instructional program. Comparison of the performance on common examinations of students who have had different instructors provides one of the most objective evaluations of the effectiveness of instruction, but the threat conveyed by this approach is not conducive to improvement. Moreover, there are so many unknowns and so many objectives for which inadequate means of appraisal are available that any definite conclusions are vulnerable. More significant evaluation of instruction takes place when the individual teacher consciously tries alternatives and continually seeks for evidence as to whether the new way is more effective than those formerly used. John Jones may never be as good a teacher as George Smith, but John Jones can be a better teacher than he himself is. It is this kind of improvement that evaluation should seek for. Evaluation of the accumulative impact of the total program encourages this emphasis. While the implications out of such a broader evaluation program cannot be specific for particular courses and particular teachers, such a program will lead many teachers to rethink their role in relationship to that of other teachers in other courses.

NEEDED EMPHASIS IN EVALUATION

To the extent that general education involves a critical re-examination of higher education and a consideration of alternate ways in which the purposes of higher education may be better achieved, there is an implication of a tentativeness in the solutions voiced which should be conducive to an experimental point of view. Such has not been the case. In a few institutions such as Antioch College, the General College of the University of Minnesota, San Francisco State College, Stephens College, and Michigan State University, continuing evaluation activity has played a role of greater or less significance in the development of the general education program. While this list could undoubtedly be extended, evaluation in most programs has been incidental, sporadic, and highly subjective in nature. Modifications and even eliminations of general education offerings have often resulted from the whim of a single individual in an administrative hierarchy without recourse to any kind of factual evidence. Experimentation and evaluation have not been the route to decision.

Such evaluation as has been done demonstrates some weaknesses. More studies are needed of the long term development of individuals with regard to some of the more significant concepts, principles, and ideals, in contrast with our current emphasis on specifics. Much to the point is the development of new and more imaginative ways of instruction and the comparison of these with our more standard practices. The extensive accumulating evidence on instruction by television is an example. More careful studies are needed of the introductory courses in the various fields to see whether indeed the specialized needs of prospective majors and the general education needs of the larger group of students involved in many of these courses are mutually exclusive. Some of the recent ventures in restudy of mathematics and physics courses at the high school and freshman year of college suggest that the materials most significant for the beginning student in the field are also precisely the kinds of thing that should be taught for general education purposes.

The economic motive in higher education has been commented upon repeatedly. While there is some evidence that students do recognize the significance of general education goals, the fact remains that too little is done in most of our colleges to interpret to students the meaning of higher education and to enlist their own interest in self-improvement. Something more needs to be done in the way of in-service training for the teaching staff to help them focus attention on the ultimate goal and to see their own course and instruction and goals in relationship to the development of the student toward that final goal. The relationship between general, technical, and specialized education needs to be further explored and clarified in the minds of both staff and students. Currently the reports of the professional societies and the work of Dr. Earl McGrath at Columbia suggest that many of the professional groups may be more aware of the significance of general education than are the liberal arts faculties.

Reference has been made to the need for exploration of new and more imaginative learning experiences. Faced with increasing enrollments, more needs to be done to arouse the student's incentive to take responsibility for his own education and to provide for him a variety of materials and facilities which may even improve rather than simply substitute for the reduced amount of instructor time per student. Increasingly, the four years of college will be broken into two lesser units of two years each. An increasing percentage of students will be taking much of their college work as commuters. The original conception of a college education as a four year period of planned and interrelated experiences is gradually disappearing. Unless some way is found to encourage the student to be concerned about the organization of his educational experiences and the accumulative impact of them, and unless some way is found to cause him to reexamine his own values and encourage him to develop his own originality and creativity, the credit accumulation aspects of higher education will become even more potent.

For some years most colleges have concentrated on revising and adding courses rather than on major curriculum restudy. If, in the face of the disintegrative forces just noted, unity is to return to higher education, it must be through total curriculum restudy. New ideas are needed and evaluation of them is a necessity. Faculties who engage in this activity will arrive at a better educational program if only by their increased awareness of and sensitivity to the complex nature of the task. Hopefully, they will also arrive at some way to achieve a new unity in the curriculum through improved teaching-learning practices which emphasize outcomes inclusive of but transcending an increase in specialized factual knowledge. What they arrive at may not be called general education, but it will be a better education. This is the end—and the beginning—of evaluation.

NOTES

[1] Bloom, B. S., & Broder, L. J., *Problem Solving Processes of College Students* (Chicago, University of Chicago Press), 1950.

[2] It is not entirely irrelevant to suggest here that the current idea that students should be charged the price of their education—even if this means borrowing funds and repaying them after college—may add another delimiting factor to this pattern.

Chapter VIII

THE FUTURE OF GENERAL EDUCATION

LEWIS B. MAYHEW
Director of Evaluation and Research,
University of South Florida,
and Director of Research, Stephens College

ONE cannot review the varieties of programs and practices in general education without being tempted to determine what it all means; and such speculation leads inexorably into attempts at predicting the future. The editor was unable to withstand the temptation. The points which will be considered are all implications in one way or another from the specific discussions in earlier chapters. The way the points are used in this forecast are, however, the responsibility of the editor alone.

General education as described in these chapters is but an aspect of collegiate education. As a subordinate part, it is bound to be affected by what happens to higher education as a whole. Hence, any view of the future must recognize some major developments in collegiate education which will determine the course of all of its subordinate aspects.

Perhaps the first of these major trends is a pendulum-like swing of educational thought to an older, more conservative outlook. Indeed, much of American society seems to have lost faith in liberal conceptions of change, improvement, and the perfectibility of man. The search for lost religious values, the desire to re-establish old-time national virtues, and the attempts to restore the sanctity of the family, are illustrative. Within collegiate education the resurgence of interest in foreign language requirements, and the increased requirements of traditional academic subjects such as mathematics and basic sciences, are reflections of the same conservative spirit. People seem to be saying that the gains from a more liberal, pragmatic philosophy of education are, apparently, increased juvenile delinquency, Russian leadership in an age of Sputnik, and accelerated use of alcohol and tranquilizing drugs by educated people. Perhaps it would be better, they think, to go back to an education which did not lead to such personal and social abnormalities.

Akin to the desire to restore traditional patterns of courses is the success which university faculties have had in emasculating divisional organization structure. As traditional departments were found too specialized to offer the kind of general education people needed, many universities established divisions which by controlling a number of related disciplines, could offer broadly conceived inter-disciplinary courses. Divisions frequently stood as a threat to traditional departments, and divisional courses curtailed seriously the subsidy for specialized research which had previously been available to departments. In previous times, introductory courses had been viewed as a way by which graduate students could be paid while they carried out the research of the graduate faculties. At such places as the University of Minnesota and the University of Louisville, professors within departments have been successful in causing a curtailment of power and finances of divisions. At other institutions which are even now creating divisions, no real authority is being granted them. The balance of academic power seems to be falling back to the independent subject department.

Certainly a keynote in the age of resurgent conservatism is a rejection of John Dewey and the entire constellation of ideas and principles which comprised progressive education. It has come to pass that the easiest way to defeat a proposal before a college faculty is to label it as progressive or as fellow-traveling with followers of Dewey. This when European scholars still view Dewey as the most characteristically American of all educational and social theorists.

A second major trend in collegiate education is the changing relationship between the two- and the four-year institution. There was a time, now apparently passing, when attending college connoted going to a four-year school. As a matter of fact, the four-year liberal arts college is a purely American institution. However, as American society has attempted to extend collegiate education to larger segments of its population, the values of the two-year, locally controlled and supported junior college have been argued. The presentation of these institutions as a remedy for the problems of college education has been spectacularly successful and, in many states, the time is not distant when the junior colleges will be educating more students in the thirteenth and fourteenth years than all of the four-year institutions combined. This situation already prevails in California and will be true in Michigan within five years.

An adjunct of this phenomenon is the growing conviction that American society should recognize differences in colleges just as it recognizes differences in individuals. In the past a college degree was regarded as a kind of badge of status, regardless of where or how acquired. It is true that initially upon graduation a badge from Harvard College or Yale might have more glamour than one from Michigan State. However, the glamour did not long distinguish between them, for within ten years after graduation the Harvard graduate could scarcely be distinguished from the State graduate, and neither differed appreciably from the adult similarly employed, who had not attended college. Of recent years such spokesmen as James B. Conant ex-president of Harvard, have argued for clear recognition that there are a few universities of excellence in the nation. These are the ones, he says, which should provide the scholarly education needed by the future leaders of the nation. Other institutions should be designated as what they are—necessary, important, but intellectually inferior people's schools. The junior colleges would, of course, fall within this category.

A third trend is an increased emphasis on the education of the gifted or able student. As a continental nation with tremendous natural resources, and as a recipient of the excess populations of the older European civilization, America has been careless in the use of both natural and human resources. With the frontier gone, with stocks of iron, oil, and minerals depleted, and with the steady influx of new vital human reserves stopped, America has suddenly awakened to the need for conservation. She has discovered that many of the brightest people are not attending college, and that of those who are, an alarming number are dropping out before gaining a definite educational goal. To provide more realistically for such students, colleges have begun to identify bright students early and to arrange courses and programs for their peculiar needs. The serious attention being paid to independent study, to honors courses, and to methods of acceleration of educational progress is illustrative of the trend.

As some of these methods have proven effective, there has come to be some experimentation with similar methods applied to students of more modest talents. One institution, for example, has established an Honors College which opens the entire curriculum for its students as well as providing them certain prerogatives not available to regular students in the other colleges. The vice-president is vitally interested in it not only for the group of students it now services, but as a possible prototype for the future total undergraduate program of the university.

A fourth trend is the increased significance of the state-supported institution in meeting the total educational needs of the nation. The time is past when private institutions have educated over half of the total number of students in college. Within a decade the present ratio of 47 per cent to 53 per cent will drop so that private colleges will be educating no more than 20 per cent of all college students in the country. With this drop in proportion will likely come a drop in public support, particularly in view of the fact that all education must function on its share of the gross national product. As more and more graduates of state schools assume positions of leadership in the community, their decisions for the allocation of funds, either through gifts or taxes, will likely favor the kind of school from which they graduated. With the resources thus obtained, public education can drain off the professional talent from the more poorly supported private schools. While most spokesmen for education claim to value pluralism in which both public and private education can exist, their claims must be viewed against major social and economic forces.

A fifth trend, which may have most dramatic consequences to education, is still so faint as scarcely to be perceptible. Social institutions exist to accomplish necessary tasks for society, which in turn reflect basic human needs. The particular functions of individual institutions mutate from time to time as cultural and technological changes come about. Thus, at one time the family had almost exclusive responsibility for the education of children and for the vocational preparation of future adults. It also was the major economically productive agency in society. Gradually it yielded those functions to other institutions. Education at one time had virtually no vocational training responsibilities except for a few critical professions. The family—and business or industry, through the apprentice system—accomplished the needed training of the young in skills of work. Gradually schools and colleges assumed larger shares of vocational training and in the past fifty years have been the major instruments for doing this work.

There is currently more than the suggestion that other institutions may be reassuming responsibility in this sphere of human activity. The military forces with their elaborate systems for providing technical training, business and industry with their growing number of technical institutes and in-service training programs, and labor unons with a complex system of educational meetings and indoctrination seminars, may be doing what schools formerly were expected to do. Such activities become especially significant when viewed in the light of pronouncements of leaders in these fields that they want generally or liberally educated recruits rather than persons highly trained in specific skills. Many such statements clearly imply that given a broadly educated person, the particular business or industry can make a skilled technician out of him.

If this trend should become pronounced, a number of important consequences could be predicted. Schools and colleges might then have the time to do what they say they can do, i.e., provide for the liberal education of the student's intellect. However, even this has risks, for if society reassigns the giving of vocational training to other agencies, it might also curtail equivalently the financial support of schools and colleges.

Another important trend which will affect the future of general education is the anticipated greater reliance on scientific methods of prediction and appraisal. It is something of a paradox that at a time of reemerging conservatism some of the methods of liberal social theory should also be accepted. Paradoxical or not, the point remains that education will make greater and greater use of a variety of tests and measures of human abilities. This point, of course, has been given statutory force, since the federal government designates money for national testing programs. As the population pressures on colleges and universities intensify, there will be greater reliance placed on tests to select from the many applicants those who will most likely profit from collegiate education. In order to insure even greater reliability, one can predict intensified use of tests to place people in appropriate courses after they have once been admitted. Further, in extension of the psychological revolution which has come about since the impact of Freud, one can predict more and more reliance on measures which probe students' opinions, values, personal adjustment, and personality structure itself.

Not only will individuals be scrutinized by more objective means of appraisal but specific institutions will also be subjected to similar techniques. The growing power of agencies of accreditation and the stimulation they have given to objective institutional self-studies are both illustrative of this trend. For example, at the present time in the North Central Association area there are over one hundred self-studies in progress. There is also a well subsidized leadership training program which is designed to produce people who can assist colleges in making such studies.

Allied to this greater use of science in measurement is a trend involving greater use of machines in teaching. Obviously, the television screen is an important aspect of this. Somewhat less well known are the devices only now coming out of psychological laboratories which can teach some things more effectively than teachers can. Devices for self-drill have produced greater gains in learning German than have accrued from greater time spent in class plus out-of-class study. The electronic devices now being used in language laboratories have produced startling results.

A last trend is the attempt on the part of education to provide for the newly acquired leisure of the American. At the present time, men must devote a relatively small amount of time to labor in order to provide the highest standard of living ever known in the history of the world. Within two decades the amount of required work can be expected to be reduced by half. How human beings are to use the time thus made available as leisure will be the responsibility of education. The time will have passed when training for the job market will be the chief function of a college. The general education movement can be viewed as one of the first responses of education to the full awareness of the leisure-using needs of people. This, of course, is no new phenomenon in world history. The early medieval universities were vocational schools to train clergy and to train lawyers for the emerging governments of the monarchs. When western society had become stable enough and men wanted more help in using leisure, the rise of humanism appeared as the answer of the school.

To these fundamental changes which appear to be taking place in American higher education must be added certain changes now occurring in general education itself. Only from these can any reasonable prediction be made for the future.

The first of these is a tendency to modify or abolish English or rhetoric or communication skills requirements. Perhaps the most widely prescribed course which could be conceived of as general education has been some form of English composition.

Frequently such a course has also been associated with another remedial offering for students deficient in language facility. Both types of courses, however, have been increasingly criticized, the remedial for being concerned with problems more rightly the province of secondary education and the English composition course on the grounds that language facility more properly should be the concern of professors in all fields. The argument runs that students have already had twelve years of formal training in language. Surely what they need, then, is application of language in academic fields rather than further drill in fundamentals. Illustrative of criticism of remedial services is the action of the University of Illinois in abolishing its sub-freshman rhetoric course. A change which is taking place at Michigan State, making the course in communications skills more of an American studies course emphasizing content rather than language skills, is illustrative of the second.

A second mutation in general education seems to be an increased emphasis on education for international awareness. Allied with this is an effort to make the content of general education less provincially tied to Western civilization. The original statements of objectives of general education contained in such things as *The Design for General Education,* or the *Report of the President's Commission on Higher Education* contained only the vague implication of responsibility for teaching young people sensitivity to foreign cultures and the abilities to function effectively abroad. Their statements seemed almost preoccupied with home and family living, with good citizenship, and with the ability to think critically about a variety of personal problems. People active in the formative period of the greatest growth in general education, the 1940's, saw scant value for foreign language in the programs they were trying to establish. However, as America's true position in the world began to be clarified, as the sheer number of Americans going abroad—as technical advisers, members of the armed services, or tourists—began to assume enormous proportions, these attitudes began to shift. In 1949, Dr. Earl McGrath, who had previously opposed foreign language, said that he might have been wrong and that he could see an important place for it in programs of general education. The American Council on Education sponsored a series of studies which led to the publication of a number of volumes on education for international understanding. More recently the National Committee on General Education of the National Education Association has devoted much of its time to devising ways to teach people to live in an international community. Similarly, Harlan Cleveland of Syracuse University studied the training of people who were abroad and obtained from them their ideas as to what training they would like to have. And these theories are being translated into practice. A number of institutions have begun to experiment with ways to provide part of a student's education abroad. Thus, Antioch has a year-abroad program and Stephens College its summer abroad. There is some speculation that the Michigan State University social science course may shift its emphasis and deliberately teach about non-European cultures in an effort to train its students for possible visits abroad.

Of a similar nature has been the movement away from an exclusive preoccupation with American and Western European culture. The major general education programs in the country taught social science either as American history or as American social problems. Courses in the humanities were typically historically oriented courses dealing with important humanistic documents in the history of the West. Many leaders in general education exemplified in practice the point of view expressed by the late Gordon Chalmers that non-European cultures had value for American education only insofar as they supported traditional Western values. This has begun to change, however, as the significance of Oriental, African, and Middle Eastern societies has loomed larger in the consciousness of Americans. While it is still too early to tell what specific developments will take place, there is discussion on many university campuses seeking ways to recognize this significance in course offerings. One proposal at Michigan State, for example, is to emphasize Western European values in the humanities course, American culture in the communication skills course, and non-occidental problems in the social science course.

A third observable change in general education programs is a growing disenchantment with courses dealing with personal adjustment. Immediately after World War II a spate of courses developed which sought to help students find themselves and their true interests. Courses such as "effective living" or "personal adjustment" seemed likely to multiply. However, few colleges were equipped to teach such courses in ways which would really make them significant in the lives of students. For example, courses dealing with personality development, vocational choice, and problems of courtship and marriage raised problems in the minds of students which demanded personal counseling finally to resolve. Ideally, such courses should have been organized so that each teacher would spend the bulk of his time counseling with individual students. Since such a course was beyond the resources of most institutions, the offering became simply descriptive of the problems typical age groups faced. Not coming to grips with students' unique problems, these personal adjustment sequences began to experience unfavorable student opinion. Coincident with their failure to enlist student support, these courses also were affected by the growing conviction that the business of the college was with the intellect alone and that an individual's adjustment was something which could not be taught in a college course. The number of these courses began to decline in number, and those which remained declined in relative importance.

At the same time that courses in personal adjustment have declined in importance, there has come a renewed interest in student values as legitimate concerns of collegiate education. Professor Philip Jacob reviewed a number of studies dealing with students' values and reached the conclusion that general education programs did not seem to affect them appreciably. He found that, with the exception of graduates of a few colleges, students' systems of values were substantially the same when they graduated from college as when they started. Further, he implied that neither he nor the rest of the teaching profession like the values which so persisted. Stimulated by the Jacob study and by intuition that something was wrong, a number of institutions have reopened the subject of teaching directly for changes in values. A group of institutions, which are attempting deliberately to affect values, sent representatives to a conference in the summer of 1958 in which the problem was discussed. The Social Science Research Council set up a new committee to study how changes in student values can be appraised and the United States Office of Education has designated some of the cooperative research funds for studies of student values. It may be that these various developments will end only in verbal expressions of concern. It may be that they will result in major curricular revisions. It is still too early to tell.

Similarly unknown is the outcome of a mounting concern for curricular integration. Many people have believed that programs of general education should contain some explicit provisions to help students relate the various aspects of their education. A majority of the institutional self-studies financed by the Ford Fund for the Advancement of Education contain strong recommendations that a senior integrating course or senior seminars or colloquia be established to this end. The National Society for the Study of Education devoted one of the 1957 yearbooks to the integration of educational experience, and an increasing number of colleges have established senior comprehensive examinations designed to facilitate integration. While there appears to be a mounting concern with integration, there also appears to be substantial uncertainty as to what integration is or whether it can be achieved through formal education. Again, only time can tell the direction this concern will eventually take.

One further dynamic element of the general education movement should be mentioned. General education in its most characteristic form has been concentrated in the first two years of college. There is presently considerable speculation as to how general education concepts, procedure, and orientation can be extended into the upper levels of the undergraduate years and even into graduate and professional schools. Such specialized fields as engineering, law, and medicine have produced reports calling for more general education in the pre-professional education of their students. Medical schools, for example, have consistently reduced the required science preparation of students enrolling in medical schools. And a few medical schools have altered some of their purely professional offerings to make them broader in conception and application. The same development is detectable in graduate schools as critics and committees have scrutinized the preparation of college teachers and found it wanting. Jacques Barzun, for example, has found graduate training too specialized and too wasteful of student time, particularly with respect to the dissertation. The Committee of Fifteen in its 1956 report reached a similar conclusion and recommended a broader, interdisciplinary training for college teachers. This, of course, is almost exactly what general education had been attempting in the undergraduate schools.

Other developments could be mentioned—such as the search for a rationale for combining physical and biological sciences, the attempts to fit newer fields such as cultural anthropology and social psychology into the general education curriculum, and the never-ending search for ways to insure closer articulation between general and specialized education. This discussion may, however, have suggested enough to provide a partial basis for prediction into the future.

In the years ahead there is likely to be increased antagonism over general education. As American society reacts to domestic and international crises, and as it finds its basic premises challenged by the achievements of other peoples, it will search for scapegoats. The reaction of the American public to Russian technological achievements is exemplary. Immediately upon the launching of Sputnik, the cry arose that the American public school system was at fault and that greater national effort should be expended on producing scientists and engineers. Similarly, the reaction of the public to such ills of American society as the increased use of narcotics, puerile television programs, and a national addiction to psychiatry has been to castigate educational practice. America is a dynamic society and it exists in a dynamic world community. As America seeks a new synthesis for its own culture, and attempts to adjust to altered world conditions in which the weak have suddenly grown strong and the dispossessed have made strident demands to possess, it will experience great stress and anxiety. The public will turn on whatever in its immediate past it feels might in some way be responsible for its tension. Since general education has been highly critical of earlier forms of education and yet is viewed as part of the background of present conditions of crisis, it will be challenged and vilified, and serious attempts will be made to excise it from educational practice. Persons engaged in general education can expect to be labeled children of John Dewey, as weak persons seeking to "water down" the curriculum, and as anti-intellectuals.

However, in spite of these criticisms, general education will continue to grow, for it is an integral part of the American tradition which came into being in response to definite social and personal needs. Nor is this idle speculation. No institution which has once established general education has removed it completely from its curriculum and from the thinking of its faculty. There have been regressions and modifications, but the idea of a broad course of studies for undergraduates persists. Further, each year sees more and more colleges adopting some form of general education as they seek to reform the undergraduate curriculum. The Ford-sponsored self-studies, with few exceptions, have ended with recommendations for general education. Not all of these recommendations have been put into practice but the intent has always been clear. So long as human knowledge expands and requires synthesis for human comprehension, so long as people spend most of their time in non-vocational activities, and so long as education believes it has responsibility for changing human behavior, the general education movement is likely to be with us.

A second prediction concerns where programs of general education are organized and who provides leadership for them. In the past the large, complicated universities first saw the need for general education as they recognized the limitations of specialized education in their own professional schools. Typically, such places as the University of Minnesota, Michigan State University, or the University of Florida, established programs for their own students. They did not attempt to foster similar programs in other colleges in their states. However, all such institutions are now facing the shrinkage of enrollments during the first two years, while those of junior colleges are expanding. Within a few years the majority of university graduates in many states will have received their first two years of college at some other institution. In order to safeguard their conceptions of the values of general education, universities will have to scrutinize more carefully the general education courses of the junior colleges from which they receive the majority of their transfer students. To use Michigan State as an example, it believes that all of its graduates should have a basic or general education. As long as it was able to educate most of its students for four years, this hope was valid. Now, however, since it must rely on junior colleges within the state for the training of its students during the first two collegiate years, it must either give up its conception of an ideal education or else exercise some influence, if not outright control, over the curricula of junior colleges. It seems most likely that the latter will happen and, further, that the same pattern will characterize other states. The condition with respect to junior colleges will not be unlike that of secondary schools a generation ago, when the colleges and universities established the criteria for judgment of secondary school curricula.

A third prediction is that the classroom will become much more significant in providing the general education of students than it ever has been in the past. Throughout most of the history of American education the values of collegiate education were seen to be achieved through the total impact of the entire college experience. Going to college implied leaving home and living in a residential collegiate community. What classes failed to accomplish, the fraternity system, organized athletics, the chapel, or the dormitory could. However, the college of the future is likely to enroll more and more students who live at home. The ideal now seems to be that there shall be a college within commuting distance for every young person in the nation. As this ideal is realized, students can be expected to come to college in the morning and leave after their last class each day. What impact the college has on them must be accomplished in classrooms. This means that there must be a greater attention to teaching procedures if classes are to assume the tremendous responsibilities so forced upon them.

This point may be further illustrated by noting the concern of residential colleges with a pattern of student behavior which has become widespread since World War II. Students leave the campus in droves on Friday afternoon and return early Monday morning. People in extracurricular activities and student personnel work are alarmed that their programs cannot be effective in the face of mass student exodus. A similar dilemma will face all other parts of the college in years ahead.

Since the classroom will grow in importance, there will be greater attention paid to the training of college teachers. The time is rapidly passing when the acquisition of a Ph.D. can be considered adequate training for college teachers. There will be courses on methods, research into teaching procedures, and a growing literature about teaching. Already there are developments which foretell this expansion of explicit concern for teaching into the college years. The new program for college teachers, the newly formed institutes for the study of higher education, and the amount of time educational meetings now give to the improvement of teaching all illustrate the trend. In the future, the training of persons to teach general education courses in the undergraduate college will become an important activity of universities.

Allied with this enhanced value assigned teaching will come greater preoccupation with the mechanics of instruction. Comprehensive examinations, placement tests, audio-visual aids, and a host of other techniques will find greater use. Very likely the lecture method of teaching will never disappear, but its primacy will be challenged by other methods even as it now is being replaced by discussion or the lecturette. These methods will not be greeted enthusiastically by many professors. They will complain, but gradually adopt them. The rate will probably be similar to the rate of acceptance of objective-type tests. Many of the most violent critics of objective appraisal now use machine-scored tests regularly. Some of this obviously is from necessity but some is clearly from choice.

One last prediction can be made. It has to do with articulation between general and vocational education. On many campuses teachers in specialized fields have conducted their courses as though required general education courses did not exist. As such departments are forced by educational, social, and economic factors to accomplish specialized training in shorter periods of time and to rely on junior colleges to prepare students who will first enter specialized training as juniors, they will concern themselves more and more with the nature of that earlier training. Circumstances will force upper level courses to build on lower level experiences in ways which were never before possible. Until now, specialized education has regarded itself as the reason for most students being in college. The traditional liberal arts courses, it should be pointed out, are, in effect, specialized education. As some of the duties of technical education are assumed by business, labor, and industry, its overall significance may decrease. To be effective at all, technical education will have to relate with—and thus extend the values of—general education.

INDEX